Effortless Mediterranean Diet Cookbook for Beginners

2100 Days of Easy, Fast, and Delicious Recipes | Includes a 60-Day Meal Plan for a Smooth Transition to Wellness | Ready in Less Than 30 Minutes

Vivian Ricci

Table of Contents

Part 1.
Embracing the Mediterranean Lifestyle

Introduction

Welcome to the vibrant world of the Mediterranean Diet, a lifestyle celebrated not only for its rich culinary traditions but also for its profound health benefits. This cookbook is designed for beginners who are eager to explore the flavorful and nutritious world of Mediterranean cooking. Whether you're seeking a healthier lifestyle, aiming to manage your weight, or simply looking to diversify your meals with fresh and wholesome ingredients, you've picked the right guide to help you on this journey.

The Mediterranean Diet isn't just a diet—it's a sustainable way of life that has evolved over thousands of years in the Mediterranean region. Recognized by nutritionists and health experts worldwide, this diet is rich in vegetables, fruits, whole grains, beans, nuts, seeds, and olive oil. It emphasizes the consumption of fish and seafood a few times a week, moderate portions of dairy products, and limited intake of red meat and sweets. What makes this diet particularly enjoyable is its flexibility and focus on flavor and variety, making it easy to adopt and maintain long-term.

What is the Mediterranean Diet?

The Mediterranean Diet is more than just a list of foods; it's a cultural heritage rooted in meals that are traditionally enjoyed in countries surrounding the Mediterranean Sea, such as Italy, Greece, Spain, and Morocco. The diet's principles are based on the dietary patterns of these regions in the 1960s, when populations displayed remarkably low chronic disease rates and higher life expectancy figures compared to other parts of the world. One of the hallmarks of the Mediterranean Diet is its emphasis on whole, minimally processed foods. This includes a high intake of vegetables and fruits, which are not only great sources of vitamins and minerals but also of fiber and antioxidants that help fight diseases. Whole grains, legumes, and nuts provide essential proteins, fats, and more fiber, which aid in digestion and provide sustained energy. Olive oil is the primary source of added fat in the Mediterranean Diet, celebrated for its heart-healthy monounsaturated fats.

Health Benefits

Adopting a Mediterranean Diet can have profound health benefits. Studies have shown that this diet significantly reduces the risk of heart disease, thanks to its emphasis on healthy fats and high-fiber foods. It's also associated with a lower risk of certain cancers, Alzheimer's disease, Parkinson's disease, and type 2 diabetes. Moreover, it's known for aiding weight loss and helping to manage weight more effectively in a pleasurable and satisfying way.

Sustainability and Pleasure

One of the most appealing aspects of the Mediterranean Diet is its focus on enjoying meals with family and friends. The diet celebrates the social aspect of eating, encouraging communal meals and sharing the joy of cooking home-prepared dishes. It's not only about what you eat but also how you eat, promoting a slower and more mindful approach to meals.

What You'll Find in This Cookbook

This cookbook is tailored for beginners and includes a variety of recipes to help you easily integrate the Mediterranean Diet into your daily life. You will find:
- Simple, straightforward recipes featuring fresh, easily accessible ingredients.
- Nutritional insights to help you understand the benefits of key ingredients.

- Tips on how to stock your pantry the Mediterranean way, ensuring that you have all the essentials for a spontaneous Mediterranean meal.
- A diverse range of dishes from simple salads and soups to more elaborate fish and seafood recipes.
- Guidelines on how to combine these dishes to create balanced meals that reflect the dietary habits of Mediterranean cultures.

Each recipe in this cookbook adheres to the core principles of the Mediterranean Diet and emphasizes simplicity and nutrition, ensuring that even those new to the kitchen can prepare meals with confidence and ease. More than just providing recipes, this book aims to imbue the spirit of Mediterranean cooking into your kitchen, making healthy eating a delightful and rewarding experience.

Embarking on Your Mediterranean Journey

As you turn the pages, be inspired to experiment with the flavors and ingredients that make Mediterranean cuisine uniquely delicious and nutritious. Remember, the Mediterranean Diet is forgiving and flexible; it's not about strict rules but rather about finding a joyful, balanced approach to eating.

Get ready to nourish your body and delight your palate! Welcome to the Mediterranean Diet, a journey of taste, health, and discovery. Let's begin this delicious adventure together!

Chapter 1: Why Choose the Mediterranean Diet?

Embarking on a new diet can be a daunting task, especially with the myriad of eating plans available today. Each promises optimal health, weight loss, and more. Yet, the Mediterranean Diet stands out not just as a temporary meal plan but as a time-tested lifestyle choice embraced by some of the world's healthiest populations. This chapter explores the compelling reasons to choose the Mediterranean Diet, from its rich cultural heritage to its scientifically backed health benefits and its favorable comparison with other diets.

1. Origins and Cultural Significance

The Mediterranean Diet is deeply rooted in the lifestyles of those who live along the Mediterranean Sea's shores, particularly in Greece, Southern Italy, Spain, and parts of North Africa and the Middle East. Unlike newer dietary fads that come and go, the Mediterranean Diet has evolved over millennia, influenced by the climate, cultural diversity, and historical interactions among the peoples of this vibrant region.

Cultural Practices and Foods:
The foundation of the diet lies in the way meals are approached: cooking from scratch with fresh, seasonal ingredients; sharing meals with family and friends; and balancing flavors and nutrition. Staples of the diet include abundant fruits and vegetables, whole grains, legumes, nuts, seeds, herbs, and spices—foods that have been grown around the Mediterranean basin for centuries. Olive oil, the cornerstone of the diet, is used abundantly for cooking and dressing dishes.

Historical Roots:
Historically, the Mediterranean Diet reflects the simple eating habits of the region's rural populations, who cultivated their land and sea resources to create hearty, wholesome meals even during times of economic hardship or scarcity. The concept of "eating what your garden grows" mirrors this diet's essence, emphasizing seasonal, local produce and minimal waste. This sustainable approach to eating is both a tradition and a necessity that has shaped the diet's development over time.

2. Proven Health Benefits

Scientific interest in the Mediterranean Diet began in the 1950s when it was observed that populations in the Mediterranean region exhibited lower incidences of chronic disease and longer lifespans compared to other parts of the world. Since then, numerous studies have confirmed the health benefits of this diet, making it one of the most recommended by nutritionists and health professionals worldwide.

Cardiovascular Health:

The diet's high content of olive oil, nuts, and fatty fish contributes to a healthy heart by reducing harmful cholesterol levels and increasing good cholesterol. These factors help prevent the build-up of fatty deposits in arteries, thereby reducing the risk of heart disease, stroke, and hypertension.

Anti-inflammatory Properties:

Chronic inflammation is linked to a host of health issues, including arthritis, Alzheimer's, and metabolic syndrome. The Mediterranean Diet, rich in antioxidants and healthy fats, naturally combats inflammation. Foods like tomatoes, nuts, and leafy greens contain essential vitamins and minerals that reduce cellular stress and inflammation.

Longevity and Preventive Care:

Adherents of the Mediterranean Diet often experience enhanced longevity. This benefit is attributed to the diet's ability to support a healthy weight, reduce the risk of type 2 diabetes, and discourage the development of obesity-related illnesses. Its focus on whole foods and healthy fats also supports brain health, potentially reducing the risk of developing cognitive decline and dementia.

3. Comparison with Other Diets

When compared to other popular diets, the Mediterranean Diet offers a unique blend of flexibility and sustainability that many find more realistic and enjoyable over the long term.

Keto and Paleo:

Unlike the high-fat, low-carb focus of the Keto diet or the restrictive nature of the Paleo diet, the Mediterranean Diet does not cut out entire food groups or require significant carbohydrate reduction. It allows a broad variety of foods in moderation, making it easier to maintain and less restrictive over time.

Vegan and Vegetarian:

While the Mediterranean Diet includes meat and fish, its principles are closely aligned with vegetarian eating, focusing heavily on plant-based foods and healthy fats. It is more flexible than a strict vegan or vegetarian diet, however, which can make it more appealing and accessible to a wider range of people.

Low-Fat Diets:

Contrary to diets that emphasize low-fat eating, the Mediterranean Diet celebrates fats—specifically healthy ones. Olive oil, nuts, and fatty fish are central to its approach, providing cardiovascular benefits that low-fat diets often miss.

In conclusion, the Mediterranean Diet offers more than just a way to lose weight—it's a pathway to a healthier and more enjoyable life. Its rich cultural roots, combined with a strong foundation in modern nutritional science, make it one of the most enjoyable, healthful, and sustainable diets available today. Whether you are looking to improve your heart health, reduce the risk of chronic disease, or simply enjoy delicious, wholesome meals, the Mediterranean Diet is a fulfilling choice.

Chapter 2: The Mediterranean Diet Pyramid

The Mediterranean Diet Pyramid serves as a visual guide to the pattern of eating that characterizes this enduring and healthful diet. Unlike more restrictive dietary frameworks, the Mediterranean Pyramid is flexible and emphasizes variety and balance. It incorporates a wide array of foods, recommending daily, weekly, and occasional consumption patterns that are easy to follow. This chapter delves into understanding the pyramid's structure, outlines the recommended intake of different food groups, and discusses the balance of macronutrients and micronutrients essential to the Mediterranean lifestyle.

1. Understanding the Diet Pyramid

The Mediterranean Diet Pyramid was developed as a collaborative effort between the Harvard School of Public Health and the World Health Organization in 1993. It was based on the dietary traditions of Greece and southern Italy during the early 1960s, updated periodically to reflect advances in nutritional science.

Structure of the Pyramid:
- Base Layer (Daily Intake): The foundation emphasizes physical activity and social meals, essential components of the Mediterranean lifestyle. Foods in this category include whole grains, fruits, vegetables, beans, herbs, spices, nuts, and healthy fats such as olive oil. These should constitute the bulk of one's diet.
- Middle Layers (Weekly Intake): Fish and seafood several times a week provide high-quality proteins and omega-3 fatty acids. Poultry, eggs, cheese, and yogurt in moderate portions are also included in this middle section, recommending moderate consumption throughout the week.
- Top Layer (Occasional Intake): Meats and sweets are at the pyramid's apex, suggesting limited consumption. Red meat should be eaten sparingly, not more than a few times a month, and sweets should be reserved for special occasions.

2. Daily and Weekly Food Intake Recommendations

Daily Recommendations:
- Vegetables: At least three to four servings where a serving could include a salad, a cup of raw leafy vegetables, or a half-cup of cooked vegetables.
- Fruits: Typically three servings of fresh fruit as snacks or desserts. Citrus fruits, apples, pears, and grapes are common choices.
- Whole Grains: Aim for around four to six servings of whole grains each day. Options include bread, cereals, pasta, and rice, preferably whole grain.
- Healthy Fats: Olive oil is the principal source of dietary fat, used for cooking and dressings. Aim for about four tablespoons daily.

Weekly Recommendations:
- Fish and Seafood: At least two servings a week of fatty fish like salmon, mackerel, and sardines which are rich in omega-3 fatty acids.

- Poultry, Eggs, and Dairy: Moderate portions several times a week. This includes small portions of cheese or yogurt daily and poultry or eggs every two days or so.
- Legumes: Beans, lentils, and other legumes are recommended at least twice a week as they are excellent protein sources, fiber, and slowly digested carbohydrates.

3. Balancing Macronutrients and Micronutrients

Macronutrients:
- Proteins: Adequate protein intake is crucial, but the Mediterranean Diet emphasizes plant-based sources and fish over red meat. Poultry, eggs, and dairy products are also included in moderation.
- Carbohydrates: Carbohydrates in the Mediterranean Diet come primarily from whole grains, fruits, and vegetables, which provide fiber and a rich array of nutrients.
- Fats: The diet is high in monounsaturated fats from olive oil and polyunsaturated fats from nuts and seafood, promoting heart health and reducing disease risk.

Micronutrients:
- Vitamins and Minerals: A varied intake of fruits, vegetables, and legumes ensures a high intake of essential vitamins and minerals, such as vitamins A, C, D, and E, as well as magnesium, iron, and potassium.
- Antioxidants: The high consumption of fruits, vegetables, nuts, and legumes also ensures a rich intake of antioxidants, which play a role in reducing oxidative stress and inflammation, contributing to the reduced risk of chronic diseases.

Balancing these macronutrients and micronutrients within the context of the Mediterranean Diet not only supports overall health but also aligns with the diet's emphasis on enjoying food in a social, relaxed setting. The diet's flexibility and focus on a variety of fresh, flavorful foods make it both enjoyable and sustainable over the long term.

In conclusion, the Mediterranean Diet Pyramid is more than a visual guide—it is a blueprint for healthy eating that emphasizes variety, moderation, and balance. Understanding and following this pyramid will help you enjoy the full benefits of the Mediterranean Diet, from a nourishing daily routine to exceptional lifelong health.

Chapter 3: Essential Ingredients

The Mediterranean Diet thrives on a diverse palette of fresh, flavorful ingredients that form the backbone of its dishes. Embracing this diet fully involves understanding these key ingredients, knowing how to source them, and learning the best practices for storage and preservation. This chapter will guide you through these essential steps, ensuring that you can make the most of the Mediterranean culinary experience.

1. Staple Foods of the Mediterranean Diet

Fruits and Vegetables:
Central to the Mediterranean diet are fruits and vegetables, which provide vitamins, minerals, fiber, and a host of antioxidants. Common staples include leafy greens like spinach and kale, Mediterranean favorites such as eggplants, artichokes, cucumbers, and a variety of tomatoes. Fruits are often enjoyed as desserts or snacks with popular choices being figs, grapes, citrus fruits, pears, and pomegranates.

Whole Grains:
Whole grains are consumed at most meals in the form of bread, pasta, rice, couscous, and other grains like barley and farro. These provide essential nutrients and fiber which help to regulate the digestive system and provide sustained energy.

Nuts and Seeds:
Nuts and seeds are integral for their protein, healthy fats, and texture. Almonds, walnuts, pistachios, pine nuts, and sesame seeds are common in the diet, either as snacks or as additions to dishes, providing crunch and flavor.

Legumes:
Beans, lentils, and chickpeas are significant sources of plant-based protein and fiber, making regular appearances in soups, stews, and salads.

Olive Oil:
Perhaps the most quintessential of Mediterranean ingredients, olive oil is the primary source of fat in the diet, used for cooking, dressings, and even as a dip.

Dairy:
Cheese and yogurt are consumed regularly but in moderate quantities. Favorites include Greek yogurt, feta, ricotta, and other soft cheeses, which are often made from sheep's or goat's milk.

Fish and Seafood:
Rich in omega-3 fatty acids, fish and seafood are vital to the diet, with salmon, sardines, mackerel, and trout being popular for their health benefits.

Herbs and Spices:
Fresh and dried herbs and spices elevate the natural flavors of foods without the need for heavy seasonings. Commonly used herbs include basil, oregano, mint, dill, parsley, and rosemary, while spices might include saffron, paprika, and cumin.

2. Shopping for Mediterranean Ingredients

To embrace the Mediterranean Diet, sourcing high-quality ingredients is key. Here's how you can shop smarter:

Local and Seasonal:
Shop at local farmers' markets for the freshest fruits and vegetables. Local produce not only tastes better but also has a higher nutritional profile due to reduced time from farm to table.

Bulk Purchases:
Buy whole grains, nuts, and legumes in bulk to save money and reduce packaging waste. Ensure that these are stored correctly to extend their shelf life.

Selecting Oils:
Choose high-quality extra virgin olive oil for the most health benefits. Look for oils in dark bottles and check the harvest date on the label to ensure freshness.

Seafood Choices:
When buying fish, opt for wild-caught over farmed if possible, as it often contains more nutrients and fewer contaminants. Check for sustainability labels to ensure responsible fishing practices.

Ethnic Markets:
For authentic ingredients like specific cheeses, spices, and olive oil, visit Mediterranean or Middle Eastern markets. These can often offer a wider variety at better prices than mainstream grocery stores.

3. Storage and Preservation Tips

Proper storage extends the life of your ingredients, keeping them flavorful and nutritious until you're ready to use them. Here are some tips:

Vegetables:
Most vegetables should be stored in the refrigerator, except for tomatoes and potatoes. Use vegetables like leafy greens within a few days, as they wilt quickly.

Fruits:
Store fruits that ripen at room temperature, such as pears and peaches, on the counter until they reach desired ripeness, then move them to the refrigerator to prolong their freshness.

Nuts and Seeds:

Because of their high oil content, nuts and seeds can go rancid quickly if not stored properly. Keep them in airtight containers in the refrigerator or freezer to extend their shelf life.

Whole Grains and Legumes:

Keep these in airtight containers in a cool, dark place. For long-term storage, you can also keep them in the freezer to preserve freshness.

Herbs and Spices:

Dry herbs and spices should be stored in airtight containers away from light and heat. Fresh herbs can last longer if they are washed, dried, and stored in the refrigerator wrapped in a damp paper towel or placed stem-side down in a cup of water.

Olive Oil:

Store olive oil in a cool, dark place away from heat sources like the stove. Olive oil can degrade in light and heat, so it's best kept in dark tinted bottles.

Understanding these essentials will not only enhance your experience with the Mediterranean Diet but also ensure that you can enjoy the most flavorful and nutritious benefits from each meal you prepare. Armed with this knowledge, you can confidently navigate the basics of Mediterranean cooking and embrace a healthier eating style with ease.

Chapter 4: The Science Behind the Diet

The Mediterranean Diet has garnered significant acclaim not only for its rich flavors and culinary diversity but also for its robust scientific backing that highlights numerous health benefits. This chapter delves into the scientific principles that underscore the Mediterranean Diet, examining its nutritional composition, its impact on cardiovascular health, and its role in weight management and metabolic health.

1. Nutritional Composition and Benefits

The Mediterranean Diet is rich in a variety of nutrients that play key roles in maintaining optimal health. Its emphasis on fruits, vegetables, whole grains, and healthy fats provides a balanced intake of macronutrients and micronutrients essential for bodily functions.

Macronutrients:
- Carbohydrates: The diet provides complex carbohydrates primarily from fruits, vegetables, and whole grains, which offer a steady source of energy and are rich in fiber. The fiber aids in digestion and helps regulate blood sugar levels.
- Proteins: Protein sources in the Mediterranean Diet include fish, poultry, beans, and legumes, providing essential amino acids without the high saturated fat content common in red meats.
- Fats: The cornerstone of the diet's fat intake is olive oil, which is high in monounsaturated fats and has been shown to reduce the risk of heart disease. Nuts, seeds, and fatty fish contribute healthful omega-3 fatty acids, which are crucial for brain health and reducing inflammation.

Micronutrients:

The diet is high in vitamins and minerals from a wide range of fruits and vegetables. For example, leafy greens are an excellent source of vitamin K, essential for bone health, while citrus fruits provide vitamin C, crucial for immune function. The variety of foods in the diet also ensures adequate intakes of minerals like iron, calcium, and magnesium.

2. Impact on Cardiovascular Health

The Mediterranean Diet is particularly renowned for its benefits to heart health. Numerous studies have linked the diet with lower levels of cardiovascular disease, including heart attacks and strokes.

Reducing Heart Disease Risk:
- Cholesterol Levels: Olive oil and nuts in the diet help lower levels of LDL (bad) cholesterol while maintaining or improving HDL (good) cholesterol levels.
- Blood Pressure: The diet's rich potassium content from fruits and vegetables helps lower blood pressure levels, a major risk factor for heart disease.
- Inflammation: The anti-inflammatory effects of the diet, credited to its rich antioxidants from fruits and vegetables, as well as omega-3 fatty acids from fish, help reduce the risk of atherosclerosis (artery hardening).

Several landmark studies, such as the Lyon Diet Heart Study and the more recent PREDIMED trial, have substantiated these effects. The PREDIMED study, in particular, noted a 30% reduction in major cardiovascular events among high-risk individuals following a Mediterranean Diet supplemented with extra virgin olive oil or nuts.

3. Weight Management and Metabolic Health

The Mediterranean Diet also supports healthy weight management and metabolic function. Unlike many restrictive diets, the Mediterranean Diet offers a sustainable approach to weight loss that emphasizes nutrient-dense, high-fiber foods which help to control appetite and reduce overall calorie intake.

Metabolic Syndrome Reduction:
- Blood Sugar Control: High fiber intake from whole grains and legumes slows the absorption of sugar, improving overall blood glucose levels and insulin sensitivity.
- Waist Circumference and Obesity: Regular consumption of plant-based foods and healthy fats helps reduce body weight and waist circumference, key factors in metabolic syndrome.

Furthermore, the diet's rich variety of plant-based foods and absence of processed foods help to modulate the gut microbiota, enhancing digestion and metabolic health. This aspect of the diet not only helps in weight management but also improves the body's overall metabolic processes, reducing the risk of developing type 2 diabetes and other metabolic conditions.

In summary, the Mediterranean Diet offers a scientifically proven approach to improving heart health, managing weight, and enhancing metabolic wellness. Its balance of nutritious foods supports sustainable health benefits that go beyond simple dietary changes, promoting long-term well-being and disease prevention. As we explore the intricate science behind this diet, it becomes clear why the Mediterranean Diet is considered one of the healthiest dietary patterns in the world.

Chapter 5: Comprehensive Health Benefits

The Mediterranean Diet is much more than a culinary tradition; it is a scientifically backed approach to eating that offers profound health benefits. These benefits extend beyond simple nutritional intake, influencing heart health, reducing the risk of numerous chronic diseases, and enhancing overall longevity and quality of life. This chapter delves into these aspects, providing a thorough understanding of how adhering to the Mediterranean Diet can lead to a healthier, more vibrant life.

1. Protecting Heart Health

Heart disease remains one of the leading causes of death globally, but the Mediterranean Diet has been shown to offer significant protections against various heart conditions. This diet emphasizes the intake of healthy fats, primarily from olive oil, nuts, and fatty fish, which are critical in managing and reducing the risk of heart disease.

Mechanisms of Heart Health Protection:
- Improved Lipid Profiles: Regular consumption of healthy fats increases HDL (good) cholesterol and decreases LDL (bad) cholesterol and triglycerides, which are crucial markers of cardiovascular risk.
- Reduced Blood Pressure: The high fiber content in fruits, vegetables, and whole grains, along with healthy fats, helps to reduce blood pressure levels, a significant risk factor for heart attacks and strokes.
- Anti-inflammatory Effects: Chronic inflammation is linked to heart disease, and the Mediterranean Diet, rich in antioxidants from fruits and vegetables and omega-3 fatty acids from fish, helps reduce inflammation throughout the body.

These effects are supported by substantial research, including longitudinal studies and randomized trials, which demonstrate that Mediterranean dietary patterns are associated with a significantly reduced risk of cardiovascular mortality and morbidity.

2. Reducing the Risk of Chronic Diseases

Beyond its cardiovascular benefits, the Mediterranean Diet is beneficial in preventing and managing other chronic diseases, including type 2 diabetes, certain cancers, and neurodegenerative diseases.

Type 2 Diabetes:
The diet's rich fiber content improves blood sugar levels and enhances insulin sensitivity, reducing the risk of developing type 2 diabetes. Studies have shown that following a Mediterranean Diet can lower the risk of developing diabetes by up to 23%.

Cancer Prevention:
The antioxidants and phytochemicals in fruits, vegetables, and whole grains provide protective effects against cancer. Regular consumption of these foods has been linked to a decreased risk of cancers, particularly colorectal, breast, and prostate cancer.

Neurodegenerative Diseases:

Dietary patterns rich in fruits, vegetables, and fatty acids from fish are associated with a reduced risk of neurodegenerative diseases like Alzheimer's and Parkinson's. The anti-inflammatory and antioxidant properties of the diet help to protect against the oxidative stress that contributes to these conditions.

3. Enhancing Longevity and Quality of Life

Perhaps one of the most compelling reasons to adopt the Mediterranean Diet is its association with increased longevity and improved quality of life. This diet not only helps people live longer but ensures that those extra years are healthier.

Mechanisms for Enhanced Longevity:

- Improved Mental Health: The diet's emphasis on whole foods and healthy fats has been shown to reduce symptoms of depression and anxiety, enhancing overall mental well-being.
- Bone Health: The nutrients found in the Mediterranean Diet, such as calcium, magnesium, and vitamin K, are vital for maintaining bone density and strength, reducing the risk of osteoporosis and fractures in older adults.
- Gut Health: High fiber intake promotes a healthy digestive system, fostering a beneficial gut microbiome, which is crucial for overall health and effective immune function.

Community and Lifestyle:

Moreover, the lifestyle associated with the Mediterranean Diet—characterized by physical activity and shared meals—plays a significant role in promoting longevity. These social and cultural aspects of eating encourage healthier eating practices and contribute to a lower level of stress and a more satisfied life.

In conclusion, the Mediterranean Diet offers extensive health benefits that encompass prevention of major chronic diseases, protection against mental decline, and enhancement of longevity and life quality. It stands out not only as a set of nutritional guidelines but as a holistic approach to long-term wellness. This diet, therefore, is not just about adding years to your life, but life to your years, making it a worthwhile choice for anyone looking to improve their health in a sustainable and enjoyable way.

Chapter 6: Lifestyle Beyond the Plate

The Mediterranean Diet is celebrated not only for its health benefits but also as a holistic lifestyle that emphasizes a balanced approach to daily living. This encompasses a variety of elements that contribute significantly to overall wellness. This chapter explores how the integration of social and cultural practices, physical activity, and mindfulness into one's routine can enrich the experience of the Mediterranean Diet and further enhance its benefits.

1. Social and Cultural Aspects

The Mediterranean lifestyle is deeply intertwined with social and cultural traditions that prioritize community, family, and shared experiences. Meals are more than just eating for sustenance; they are an opportunity for connection and celebration with others.

Communal Meals:
In Mediterranean cultures, meals are typically consumed with family or community members. This practice not only enhances social bonds but also influences the manner and pace at which food is consumed. Eating with others tends to slow down the meal, encouraging more mindful eating practices which can lead to better digestion and satisfaction with smaller portions.

Food as a Celebration:
Food in the Mediterranean is often associated with celebration and festivity. Traditional festivals and family gatherings revolve around the preparation and enjoyment of food. This association between food and happiness contributes to a positive attitude towards eating and nutrition.

Cultural Diversity of Food:
The Mediterranean region is rich in cultural diversity, and this is reflected in its cuisine. The diet varies significantly from one area to another, influenced by local customs, traditions, and the availability of different ingredients. This diversity ensures a wide array of foods in the diet, which not only prevents dietary boredom but also encourages a broader intake of nutrients.

2. Physical Activity and Exercise

Physical activity is a cornerstone of the Mediterranean lifestyle. The natural landscapes of the region—ranging from mountains to coastal areas—along with the temperate climate, encourage an active lifestyle.

Daily Physical Activities:
Historically, people living in the Mediterranean are engaged in high levels of physical activity integrated into daily life, whether through farming, walking, or cycling. This ongoing physical engagement is one of the critical factors in the health benefits associated with the diet.

Exercise as a Social Activity:
In Mediterranean cultures, exercise is often a social activity, such as walking with friends or family after dinner, which is a common practice. This not only aids digestion but also strengthens community and familial ties.

Structured Exercise:
While daily activity is important, structured exercise also plays a role. Many Mediterranean communities incorporate forms of exercise that balance physical activity with relaxation and social interaction, such as yoga, Pilates, dancing, or swimming.

3. Mindfulness and Stress Reduction

Mindfulness and stress reduction are integral to the Mediterranean lifestyle, influencing eating habits and general well-being. The slower pace of life, emphasis on joy and relaxation, and the natural surroundings help cultivate a mindful approach to life and eating.

Mindful Eating:
Mindfulness in eating—paying full attention to the experience of eating and drinking—is naturally practiced in the Mediterranean diet. Meals are often long and enjoyed without the distractions of technology or the rush of fast food.

Stress Reduction Techniques:
Mediterranean cultures have various practices to reduce stress, which can significantly impact overall health. These include siestas (short naps) in the middle of the day, spending time in nature, and engaging in hobbies or crafts that relax the mind and body.

Integration of Mindfulness in Daily Routine:
Beyond just eating, mindfulness is incorporated into daily life, allowing for a more thoughtful approach to everyday activities, which enhances mental health and reduces the risk of stress-related illnesses.

In conclusion, the Mediterranean Diet transcends the simple concept of dieting and is deeply rooted in a lifestyle that promotes overall health, happiness, and well-being. By adopting not just the eating habits but also the social customs, physical activities, and mindfulness practices of the Mediterranean lifestyle, individuals can achieve a more comprehensive approach to health that goes well beyond the plate. This holistic approach not only enhances physical health but also supports mental and emotional well-being, contributing to a richer, more fulfilled life.

Chapter 7: 60 Day Meal Plan

	Breakfast	Lunch	Dinner
Day 1	Mediterranean Smoothie Bowl	Vegan Greek Salad	Beef Stroganoff
Day 2	Stuffed Zucchini Boats	Quinoa and Vegetable Salad	Mediterranean Lentil Meatballs
Day 3	Smoked Salmon and Cream Cheese Bagel	Grilled Vegetable and Hummus Wrap	Roast Chicken with Vegetables
Day 4	Vegan Ceviche	Tuscan White Bean Soup	Cauliflower and Turmeric Soup
Day 5	Eggplant and Tomato Bake	Artichoke and Spinach Salad	Butternut Squash and Chickpea Stew
Day 6	Cucumber and Hummus Plate	Mediterranean Vegan Burger	Honey Mustard Turkey Cutlets
Day 7	Tomato and Basil Bruschetta	Parmesan Crusted Chicken	Vegan Ratatouille
Day 8	Greek Yogurt with Honey and Nuts	Vegan Stuffed Peppers	Zucchini and Basil Velouté
Day 9	Berry and Nuts Overnight Oats	Mediterranean Lentil Meatballs	Rosemary Garlic Lamb Chops
Day 10	Almond and Date Energy Balls	Roasted Vegetable Couscous	Chickpea and Spinach Stew
Day 11	Spinach and Goat Cheese Quiche	Honey Mustard Turkey Cutlets	Mediterranean Vegetable Paella
Day 12	Avocado Chocolate Mousse	Spinach and Pine Nut Pasta	Beef and Vegetable Stir-Fry
Day 13	Honey Lime Quinoa Fruit Salad	Mediterranean Shrimp Skillet	Tomato Basil Soup
Day 14	Quinoa Tabbouleh	Falafel with Tahini Sauce	Spanish Chicken and Rice

Day 15	Mediterranean Breakfast Wrap	Broccoli and Chickpea Salad	Butternut Squash and Sage Soup
Day 16	Baked Pear with Cinnamon	Baked Falafel	Grilled Tuna Steaks
Day 17	Cottage Cheese and Peach Bowl	Vegan Greek Salad	French Onion Soup
Day 18	Greek Stuffed Tomatoes (Gemista)	Spinach and Ricotta Stuffed Shells	Lemon Herb Roasted Turkey
Day 19	Shakshuka	Simple Grilled Swordfish	Baked Cod with Cherry Tomatoes and Olives
Day 20	Broccoli and Chickpea Salad	Crab Stuffed Avocado	Italian Herb Chicken
Day 21	Almond Butter and Banana Smoothie	Turkish Beef Kebabs	Grilled Salmon with Dill and Lemon
Day 22	Almond and Date Energy Balls	Sardines Grilled with Herbs	Moroccan Spiced Lamb Stew
Day 23	Carrot and Orange Salad	Grilled Vegetable and Hummus Wrap	Mediterranean Shrimp Skillet
Day 24	Spinach and Mushroom Frittata	Baked Fish with Olives and Capers	Seafood Paella
Day 25	Mediterranean Lentil Salad	Parmesan Crusted Chicken	Moroccan Lentil Stew
Day 26	Quinoa Fruit Salad	Chickpea Salad	Grilled Tuna with Olive Tapenade
Day 27	Mediterranean Omelette	Chicken and Artichoke Heart Skillet	Greek Lemon Chicken Soup
Day 28	Avocado and Tomato Salad	Fish Tacos with Cabbage Slaw	Lentil Soup
Day 29	Avocado and Tomato Toast	Mediterranean Vegan Burger	Lemon Garlic Mussels

Day 30	Nicoise Salad	Mediterranean Turkey Burgers	Spicy Tomato and Red Pepper Soup
Day 31	Smoked Salmon and Cream Cheese Bagel	Garlic and Oil Spaghetti (Aglio e Olio)	Poached Fish in Tomato Basil Sauce
Day 32	Eggplant and Tomato Bake	Classic Greek Salad	White Bean and Kale Stew
Day 33	Greek Yogurt with Honey and Walnuts	Spinach and Pine Nut Pasta	Barley and Mushroom Stew
Day 34	Roasted Vegetable Couscous	Spicy Grilled Shrimp	Herb-Crusted Pork Tenderloin
Day 35	Mediterranean Chickpea Salad	Falafel with Tahini Sauce	Broccoli and Anchovy Pasta
Day 36	Mediterranean Morning Scramble	Vegan Stuffed Peppers	Vegan Ratatouille
Day 37	Mediterranean Black Bean Salad	Parmesan Crusted Chicken	Roasted Red Pepper Pasta
Day 38	Vegan Ceviche	Tuscan White Bean Pasta	Mediterranean Vegetable Paella
Day 39	Roasted Vegetable Salad	Caprese Pasta Salad	Roasted Halibut with Fennel and Potatoes
Day 40	Watermelon and Feta Salad	Mediterranean Vegan Burger	Pumpkin and Sage Risotto
Day 41	Mediterranean Smoothie Bowl	Tuscan White Bean Soup	Clam Linguine
Day 42	Beet and Goat Cheese Salad	Spiced Chickpea Wraps	Walnut and Blue Cheese Risotto
Day 43	Tomato and Basil Bruschetta	Grilled Vegetable and Hummus Wrap	Creamy Mushroom Risotto
Day 44	Cucumber and Yogurt Salad (Cacik)	Spinach and Artichoke Pasta	Spanish Seafood Stew

Day 45	Nicoise Salad	Mediterranean Octopus Salad	Seared Scallops with Lemon Butter Sauce
Day 46	Spinach and Goat Cheese Quiche	Pesto Pasta with Grilled Chicken	Pumpkin and Cinnamon Soup
Day 47	Spinach and Strawberry Salad	Moroccan Lentil Salad	Italian Minestrone
Day 48	Berry and Nuts Overnight Oats	Greek Lemon Chicken	Butternut Squash Risotto
Day 49	Mediterranean Breakfast Wrap	Bean and Spinach Tacos	Beetroot and Potato Soup
Day 50	Carrot and Orange Salad	Zucchini Ribbon Pasta	Crab Stuffed Avocado
Day 51	Greek Yogurt with Honey and Nuts	Sardines Grilled with Herbs	Classic Tomato Risotto
Day 52	Shakshuka	Turkish Beef Kebabs	Mediterranean Lentil Stew
Day 53	Mediterranean Lentil Salad	Spinach and Ricotta Stuffed Shells	Italian White Bean Soup
Day 54	Almond Butter and Banana Smoothie	Baked Falafel	Simple Grilled Swordfish
Day 55	Avocado and Tomato Salad	Quinoa and Vegetable Salad	Asparagus Lemon Risotto
Day 56	Greek Stuffed Tomatoes (Gemista)	Mediterranean Vegetable Pasta	Carrot and Coriander Soup
Day 57	Crab Stuffed Avocado	Vegan Greek Salad	Smoky Black Bean Chili
Day 58	Mediterranean Omelette	Three-Bean Salad	Lemon Garlic Shrimp Risotto
Day 59	Broccoli and Chickpea Salad	Tomato Basil Pasta	Sweet Potato and Ginger Soup

| Day 60 | Avocado and Tomato Toast | Smoked Trout Salad | Spinach and Chickpea Curry |

Part 2.
Mediterranean
Recipes

Energizing Breakfast Recipes

1. Mediterranean Morning Scramble

- Preparation Time: 10 minutes
- Cooking Time: 5 minutes
- Servings: 2

Ingredients:

- 4 eggs
- 1 cup spinach, fresh
- ½ cup cherry tomatoes, halved
- ¼ cup feta cheese, crumbled
- 2 tbsp olives, sliced
- 1 tbsp olive oil
- Salt and pepper, to taste

Directions:

1. Heat olive oil in a skillet over medium heat.
2. Add spinach and tomatoes; sauté until spinach is wilted.
3. Beat eggs and pour them into the skillet, stirring gently.
4. When the eggs start to set, add feta cheese and olives.
5. Season with salt and pepper and cook until eggs are fully set.
6. Serve warm.

2. Greek Yogurt with Honey and Walnuts

- Preparation Time: 5 minutes
- Cooking Time: 0 minutes
- Servings: 1

Ingredients:

- 1 cup Greek yogurt
- 2 tbsp honey
- ¼ cup walnuts, chopped
- A sprinkle of cinnamon (optional)

Directions:

1. Place Greek yogurt in a bowl.
2. Drizzle honey over the yogurt.
3. Top with chopped walnuts and a sprinkle of cinnamon.
4. Serve immediately.

3. Avocado and Tomato Toast

- Preparation Time: 5 minutes
- Cooking Time: 2 minutes
- Servings: 2

Ingredients:

- 2 slices of whole grain bread
- 1 ripe avocado
- 1 tomato, sliced
- Salt and pepper, to taste
- Olive oil (for drizzling)

Directions:

1. Toast the bread slices to your liking.
2. Mash the avocado and spread it evenly on each slice of toast.
3. Top with sliced tomato.
4. Season with salt and pepper and drizzle with olive oil.
5. Serve immediately.

4. Mediterranean Omelette

- Preparation Time: 10 minutes
- Cooking Time: 5 minutes
- Servings: 1

Ingredients:

- 3 eggs
- 1/4 cup onions, diced
- 1/4 cup bell peppers, diced
- 1/4 cup tomatoes, diced
- 1/4 cup spinach
- 1/4 cup feta cheese, crumbled
- 1 tbsp olive oil
- Salt and pepper, to taste

Directions:

1. In a mixing bowl, whisk the eggs with salt and pepper.
2. Heat olive oil in a skillet over medium heat.
3. Sauté onions, bell peppers, and tomatoes until soft.
4. Add spinach and cook until wilted.
5. Pour the eggs over the vegetables in the skillet.
6. Sprinkle feta cheese on top.
7. Cook until the eggs are set and fold the omelette in half.
8. Serve hot.

5. Quinoa Fruit Salad

- Preparation Time: 10 minutes
- Cooking Time: 15 minutes
- Servings: 2

Ingredients:

- 1 cup quinoa
- 2 cups water
- 1 cup mixed berries (strawberries, blueberries, raspberries)
- 1 banana, sliced
- 1 apple, chopped
- Juice of 1 lemon
- 1 tbsp honey
- Mint leaves for garnish

Directions:

1. Rinse quinoa under cold water.
2. In a saucepan, bring water to a boil and add quinoa. Reduce heat to low, cover, and simmer for 15 minutes.
3. Let quinoa cool and then fluff with a fork.
4. In a large bowl, combine cooled quinoa, mixed berries, banana, and apple.
5. In a small bowl, whisk together lemon juice and honey.
6. Pour the dressing over the salad and toss gently.
7. Garnish with mint leaves.
8. Serve chilled or at room temperature.

6. Spinach and Mushroom Frittata

- Preparation Time: 10 minutes
- Cooking Time: 20 minutes
- Servings: 4

Ingredients:

- 6 eggs
- 1 cup fresh spinach
- 1 cup mushrooms, sliced
- 1/2 cup onions, chopped
- 1/4 cup parmesan cheese, grated
- 2 tbsp olive oil
- Salt and pepper, to taste

Directions:

1. Preheat oven to 375°F (190°C).
2. In a skillet, heat olive oil over medium heat. Sauté onions and mushrooms until they are soft.
3. Add spinach and cook until wilted.

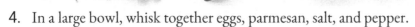

4. In a large bowl, whisk together eggs, parmesan, salt, and pepper.
5. Add the cooked vegetables to the egg mixture and stir to combine.
6. Pour the mixture into a greased baking dish.
7. Bake in the preheated oven for 20 minutes, or until the eggs are set.
8. Serve warm.

7. Almond Butter and Banana Smoothie

- Preparation Time: 5 minutes
- Cooking Time: 0 minutes
- Servings: 1

Ingredients:
- 1 banana
- 2 tbsp almond butter
- 1 cup almond milk
- 1/2 tsp vanilla extract
- Ice cubes

Directions:
1. Combine all ingredients in a blender.
2. Blend until smooth.
3. Serve immediately.

8. Shakshuka

- Preparation Time: 10 minutes
- Cooking Time: 25 minutes
- Servings: 2

Ingredients:
- 4 eggs
- 1 can (14 oz) diced tomatoes
- 1 onion, chopped
- 1 bell pepper, chopped
- 2 cloves garlic, minced
- 1 tsp cumin
- 1 tsp paprika
- 1/2 tsp chili powder
- 2 tbsp olive oil
- Salt and pepper, to taste
- Fresh cilantro, for garnish

Directions:

1. Heat olive oil in a large skillet over medium heat.
2. Add onion and bell pepper, cook until softened.
3. Stir in garlic, cumin, paprika, and chili powder; cook for 1 minute.
4. Pour in diced tomatoes and season with salt and pepper. Simmer for 10 minutes.
5. Make four wells in the tomato mixture and crack an egg into each.
6. Cover the skillet and cook until eggs are set to your liking.
7. Garnish with cilantro and serve hot.

9. Cottage Cheese and Peach Bowl

- Preparation Time: 5 minutes
- Cooking Time: 0 minutes
- Servings: 1

Ingredients:

- 1 cup cottage cheese
- 1 peach, sliced
- 1 tbsp honey
- A sprinkle of cinnamon

Directions:

1. Place cottage cheese in a serving bowl.
2. Top with sliced peach.
3. Drizzle honey over the top.
4. Sprinkle with cinnamon.
5. Serve immediately.

10. Mediterranean Breakfast Wrap

- Preparation Time: 10 minutes
- Cooking Time: 5 minutes
- Servings: 2

Ingredients:

- 2 whole grain wraps
- 4 eggs, scrambled
- 1 avocado, sliced
- 1/2 cup arugula
- 1/4 cup feta cheese, crumbled
- 2 tbsp tzatziki sauce
- Salt and pepper, to taste

Directions:

1. Lay out the wraps on a flat surface.
2. Spread each wrap with tzatziki sauce.

3. Top with scrambled eggs, avocado slices, arugula, and crumbled feta.
4. Season with salt and pepper.
5. Roll up the wraps tightly.
6. Serve immediately or wrap in foil for a to-go breakfast.

11. Honey Lime Quinoa Fruit Salad

- Preparation Time: 10 minutes
- Cooking Time: 15 minutes
- Servings: 4

Ingredients:
- 1 cup quinoa
- 2 cups water
- 2 cups fresh fruit (mango, pineapple, strawberries, kiwi)
- Juice of 1 lime
- 2 tbsp honey
- Fresh mint leaves for garnish

Directions:
1. Rinse quinoa under cold running water.
2. In a medium saucepan, bring 2 cups of water to a boil. Add quinoa, reduce heat to low, cover, and simmer for 15 minutes or until water is absorbed.
3. Remove from heat and let stand covered for 5 minutes. Fluff with a fork and allow to cool.
4. In a large bowl, combine cooled quinoa with chopped fresh fruit.
5. In a small bowl, whisk together lime juice and honey.
6. Pour dressing over quinoa and fruit mixture and toss to combine.
7. Garnish with mint leaves.
8. Serve chilled or at room temperature.

12. Spinach and Goat Cheese Quiche

- Preparation Time: 15 minutes
- Cooking Time: 35 minutes
- Servings: 6

Ingredients:
- 1 pre-made pie crust
- 4 eggs
- 1 cup milk
- 1 cup fresh spinach, chopped
- 1/2 cup goat cheese, crumbled
- 1/4 cup onions, diced
- Salt and pepper, to taste
- 1 tbsp olive oil

Directions:

1. Preheat the oven to 350°F (175°C).
2. In a skillet, heat olive oil over medium heat. Sauté onions until translucent.
3. Add spinach and cook until wilted. Remove from heat.
4. In a large bowl, whisk together eggs, milk, salt, and pepper.
5. Stir in the sautéed spinach and onions.
6. Pour the egg mixture into the pie crust.
7. Sprinkle goat cheese evenly over the top.
8. Bake in preheated oven for 35 minutes, or until the center is set.
9. Let cool for a few minutes before serving.

13. Berry and Nuts Overnight Oats

- Preparation Time: 10 minutes
- Cooking Time: 0 minutes
- Servings: 1

Ingredients:

- 1/2 cup rolled oats
- 1/2 cup almond milk
- 1/2 cup mixed berries (fresh or frozen)
- 1/4 cup nuts (walnuts, almonds)
- 1 tbsp chia seeds
- 1 tbsp honey

Directions:

1. In a mason jar or airtight container, combine oats, almond milk, chia seeds, and honey.
2. Add the mixed berries and nuts on top.
3. Close the lid and refrigerate overnight.
4. In the morning, stir the oats well and enjoy cold.

14. Tomato and Basil Bruschetta

- Preparation Time: 10 minutes
- Cooking Time: 5 minutes
- Servings: 2

Ingredients:

- 4 slices of whole-grain baguette
- 2 tomatoes, chopped
- 1 clove garlic, minced
- 6 basil leaves, chopped
- 2 tbsp olive oil
- Salt and pepper, to taste

Directions:
1. Toast the baguette slices until golden and crisp.
2. In a bowl, combine chopped tomatoes, minced garlic, chopped basil, olive oil, salt, and pepper.
3. Spoon the tomato mixture onto the toasted baguette slices.
4. Serve immediately.

15. Cucumber and Hummus Plate

- Preparation Time: 5 minutes
- Cooking Time: 0 minutes
- Servings: 1

Ingredients:
- 1 large cucumber, sliced
- 1/2 cup hummus
- Paprika, for garnish
- Olive oil, for drizzling

Directions:
1. Arrange cucumber slices on a plate.
2. Place a bowl of hummus in the center.
3. Sprinkle hummus with paprika and drizzle with olive oil.
4. Serve as a refreshing and healthy breakfast or snack.

16. Smoked Salmon and Cream Cheese Bagel

- Preparation Time: 5 minutes
- Cooking Time: 2 minutes
- Servings: 1

Ingredients:
- 1 whole grain bagel, halved and toasted
- 2 oz smoked salmon
- 2 tbsp cream cheese
- 1 tbsp capers
- 1/4 red onion, thinly sliced
- Fresh dill, for garnish

Directions:
1. Spread cream cheese on each half of the toasted bagel.
2. Layer smoked salmon over the cream cheese.
3. Top with capers and red onion slices.
4. Garnish with fresh dill.
5. Serve immediately for a savory breakfast.

17. Mediterranean Smoothie Bowl

- Preparation Time: 10 minutes
- Cooking Time: 0 minutes
- Servings: 1

Ingredients:

- 1/2 cup Greek yogurt
- 1/2 banana
- 1/4 cup frozen berries
- 1/4 cup granola
- 1 tbsp almond butter
- 1 tbsp honey
- A sprinkle of chia seeds

Directions:

1. In a blender, combine Greek yogurt, banana, frozen berries, almond butter, and honey. Blend until smooth.
2. Pour the smoothie into a bowl.
3. Top with granola and a sprinkle of chia seeds.
4. Serve immediately for a nourishing start to the day.

Delicious Pasta and Risottos

1. Tomato Basil Pasta

- Preparation Time: 10 minutes
- Cooking Time: 15 minutes
- Servings: 4

Ingredients:

- 12 oz whole wheat spaghetti
- 2 cups cherry tomatoes, halved
- 3 cloves garlic, minced
- 1/4 cup fresh basil, chopped
- 1/4 cup extra-virgin olive oil
- Salt and pepper, to taste
- Parmesan cheese, grated (optional)

Directions:

1. Cook spaghetti according to package instructions until al dente.
2. In a large skillet, heat olive oil over medium heat. Sauté garlic until fragrant.
3. Add cherry tomatoes and cook until they are soft and juicy.
4. Drain spaghetti and add to the skillet with tomatoes.
5. Toss everything together and heat through.
6. Remove from heat and stir in fresh basil.
7. Season with salt and pepper.
8. Serve with grated Parmesan if desired.

2. Lemon Garlic Shrimp Risotto

- Preparation Time: 10 minutes
- Cooking Time: 30 minutes
- Servings: 4

Ingredients:

- 1 lb shrimp, peeled and deveined
- 1 cup Arborio rice
- 4 cups vegetable broth, warmed
- 1 lemon, zest and juice
- 4 cloves garlic, minced
- 1 onion, finely chopped
- 1/4 cup white wine
- 2 tbsp olive oil
- 1/4 cup Parmesan cheese, grated
- Salt and pepper, to taste

- Fresh parsley, chopped for garnish

Directions:

1. In a large skillet, heat 1 tablespoon of olive oil over medium heat. Add shrimp and cook until pink and opaque. Remove shrimp and set aside.
2. In the same skillet, add another tablespoon of olive oil. Sauté onion and garlic until translucent.
3. Add Arborio rice and stir until the grains are well coated and start to turn translucent.
4. Deglaze the pan with white wine and let it reduce slightly.
5. Add warm vegetable broth one ladle at a time, stirring continuously, allowing each ladle to be absorbed before adding the next.
6. Once the rice is tender and creamy, stir in lemon zest, lemon juice, and cooked shrimp.
7. Mix in Parmesan cheese and season with salt and pepper.
8. Garnish with fresh parsley before serving.

3. Mediterranean Vegetable Pasta

- Preparation Time: 15 minutes
- Cooking Time: 20 minutes
- Servings: 4

Ingredients:

- 12 oz penne pasta, whole wheat
- 1 zucchini, sliced
- 1 bell pepper, sliced
- 1/2 cup sun-dried tomatoes, chopped
- 1/2 cup artichoke hearts, chopped
- 1/4 cup black olives, sliced
- 3 tbsp capers
- 1/4 cup extra-virgin olive oil
- 2 cloves garlic, minced
- Salt and pepper, to taste
- Fresh basil, for garnish

Directions:

1. Cook penne pasta according to package instructions until al dente.
2. In a large skillet, heat olive oil over medium heat. Sauté garlic until fragrant.
3. Add zucchini and bell pepper, cooking until they begin to soften.
4. Stir in sun-dried tomatoes, artichoke hearts, olives, and capers. Cook for a few minutes until heated through.
5. Drain pasta and add to the skillet, tossing to combine with the vegetables.
6. Season with salt and pepper.
7. Garnish with fresh basil and serve.

4. Asparagus Lemon Risotto

- Preparation Time: 10 minutes
- Cooking Time: 25 minutes
- Servings: 4

Ingredients:
- 1 cup Arborio rice
- 1 lb asparagus, trimmed and cut into pieces
- 4 cups vegetable broth, warmed
- 1 lemon, zest and juice
- 1 onion, finely chopped
- 1/4 cup Parmesan cheese, grated
- 2 tbsp olive oil
- Salt and pepper, to taste
- Fresh parsley, for garnish

Directions:
1. In a large pan, heat olive oil over medium heat. Sauté onion until translucent.
2. Add Arborio rice and stir for a few minutes until the grains are well coated.
3. Gradually add warm vegetable broth one ladle at a time, stirring continuously. Wait until each addition is almost fully absorbed before adding the next.
4. Halfway through, add the asparagus pieces.
5. Continue adding broth until the rice is creamy and al dente. Stir in lemon zest and juice.
6. Remove from heat and stir in Parmesan cheese. Season with salt and pepper.
7. Garnish with fresh parsley and serve.

5. Spinach and Ricotta Stuffed Shells

- Preparation Time: 20 minutes
- Cooking Time: 25 minutes
- Servings: 4

Ingredients:
- 24 jumbo pasta shells
- 1 cup ricotta cheese
- 1 cup spinach, cooked and squeezed dry
- 2 cups marinara sauce
- 1/2 cup mozzarella cheese, shredded
- 1/4 cup Parmesan cheese, grated
- 1 egg
- Salt and pepper, to taste
- Fresh basil, for garnish

Directions:

1. Preheat the oven to 375°F (190°C).
2. Cook pasta shells according to package directions until al dente. Drain and set aside.
3. In a mixing bowl, combine ricotta cheese, spinach, Parmesan cheese, egg, salt, and pepper.
4. Stuff each pasta shell with the spinach and ricotta mixture.
5. Spread a thin layer of marinara sauce in the bottom of a baking dish.
6. Arrange stuffed shells in the dish. Cover with remaining marinara sauce.
7. Sprinkle mozzarella cheese over the top.
8. Cover with foil and bake for 25 minutes. Remove foil and bake for an additional 5 minutes or until cheese is bubbly.
9. Garnish with fresh basil and serve.

6. Classic Tomato Risotto

- Preparation Time: 10 minutes
- Cooking Time: 25 minutes
- Servings: 4

Ingredients:

- 1 cup Arborio rice
- 1 can (14 oz) diced tomatoes
- 1 onion, finely chopped
- 4 cups vegetable broth, warmed
- 1/4 cup Parmesan cheese, grated
- 2 tbsp olive oil
- Salt and pepper, to taste
- Fresh basil, for garnish

Directions:

1. In a large pan, heat olive oil over medium heat. Add onion and sauté until translucent.
2. Add Arborio rice and stir to coat in the oil.
3. Gradually add warm vegetable broth, one ladle at a time, stirring continuously. Allow each addition to be absorbed before adding the next.
4. Stir in diced tomatoes with their juice halfway through cooking.
5. Once the rice is creamy and al dente, remove from heat. Stir in Parmesan cheese. Season with salt and pepper.
6. Garnish with fresh basil and serve.

7. Zucchini Ribbon Pasta

- Preparation Time: 10 minutes
- Cooking Time: 10 minutes
- Servings: 4

Ingredients:

- 12 oz spaghetti, whole wheat
- 2 zucchinis, cut into ribbons with a vegetable peeler
- 1/4 cup sun-dried tomatoes, chopped
- 1/4 cup pine nuts
- 2 cloves garlic, minced
- 1/4 cup extra-virgin olive oil
- Salt and pepper, to taste
- Fresh basil, for garnish
- Parmesan cheese, grated (optional)

Directions:

1. Cook spaghetti according to package instructions until al dente.
2. While pasta cooks, heat olive oil in a large skillet over medium heat. Add garlic and sauté until fragrant.
3. Add zucchini ribbons and sun-dried tomatoes. Cook until zucchini is tender.
4. Drain pasta and add to the skillet. Toss to combine with zucchini and tomatoes.
5. Toast pine nuts in a dry skillet until golden and add to pasta.
6. Season with salt and pepper.
7. Garnish with fresh basil and serve with grated Parmesan if desired.

8. Butternut Squash Risotto

- Preparation Time: 15 minutes
- Cooking Time: 30 minutes
- Servings: 4

Ingredients:

- 1 butternut squash, peeled and cubed
- 1 cup Arborio rice
- 4 cups vegetable broth, warmed
- 1 onion, finely chopped
- 1/4 cup Parmesan cheese, grated
- 2 tbsp olive oil
- Salt and pepper, to taste
- Fresh sage, for garnish

Directions:

1. In a large pan, heat one tablespoon of olive oil over medium heat. Add butternut squash and sauté until tender and lightly caramelized. Remove and set aside.
2. In the same pan, add the remaining olive oil and sauté onion until translucent.
3. Add Arborio rice and stir to coat with oil.
4. Gradually add warm vegetable broth, one ladle at a time, stirring constantly. Allow each addition to be absorbed before adding the next.
5. Halfway through, add the cooked butternut squash back into the pan.

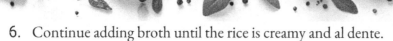

6. Continue adding broth until the rice is creamy and al dente.
7. Remove from heat, stir in Parmesan cheese, and season with salt and pepper.
8. Garnish with fresh sage and serve.

9. Pesto Pasta with Grilled Chicken

- Preparation Time: 15 minutes
- Cooking Time: 20 minutes
- Servings: 4

Ingredients:

- 12 oz whole wheat penne
- 2 chicken breasts, grilled and sliced
- 1/2 cup homemade or store-bought pesto
- 1/4 cup sun-dried tomatoes, chopped
- 1/4 cup Parmesan cheese, grated
- 2 tbsp pine nuts
- Salt and pepper, to taste

Directions:

1. Cook penne pasta according to package instructions until al dente.
2. While pasta cooks, grill chicken breasts until cooked through and slice.
3. Drain pasta and return to pot. Stir in pesto and sun-dried tomatoes.
4. Add sliced grilled chicken and toss to combine.
5. Toast pine nuts in a dry skillet until golden and sprinkle over pasta.
6. Season with salt and pepper.
7. Serve with grated Parmesan cheese.

10. Creamy Mushroom Risotto

- Preparation Time: 10 minutes
- Cooking Time: 30 minutes
- Servings: 4

Ingredients:

- 1 cup Arborio rice
- 1 lb mushrooms, sliced
- 4 cups vegetable broth, warmed
- 1 onion, finely chopped
- 1/4 cup Parmesan cheese, grated
- 2 tbsp olive oil
- 2 cloves garlic, minced
- Salt and pepper, to taste
- Fresh parsley, for garnish

Directions:

1. In a large pan, heat olive oil over medium heat. Add onion and garlic and sauté until translucent.
2. Add mushrooms and cook until they release their juices and begin to brown.
3. Add Arborio rice and stir to coat with the mushroom mixture.
4. Gradually add warm vegetable broth, one ladle at a time, stirring continuously. Allow each addition to be absorbed before adding the next.
5. Once the rice is creamy and al dente, remove from heat. Stir in Parmesan cheese. Season with salt and pepper.
6. Garnish with fresh parsley and serve.

11. Spinach and Artichoke Pasta

- Preparation Time: 10 minutes
- Cooking Time: 20 minutes
- Servings: 4

Ingredients:

- 12 oz whole wheat fettuccine
- 1 cup canned artichoke hearts, drained and chopped
- 1 cup spinach, fresh or frozen
- 1/2 cup cream cheese
- 1/4 cup Parmesan cheese, grated
- 2 cloves garlic, minced
- 2 tbsp olive oil
- Salt and pepper, to taste

Directions:

1. Cook fettuccine according to package instructions until al dente.
2. While pasta cooks, heat olive oil in a large skillet over medium heat. Add garlic and sauté until fragrant.
3. Add artichoke hearts and spinach. Cook until spinach is wilted and artichokes are heated through.
4. Reduce heat to low and stir in cream cheese until melted and smooth.
5. Drain pasta and add to the skillet, tossing to coat with the spinach and artichoke sauce.
6. Stir in Parmesan cheese and season with salt and pepper.
7. Serve immediately.

12. Walnut and Blue Cheese Risotto

- Preparation Time: 10 minutes
- Cooking Time: 30 minutes
- Servings: 4

Ingredients:

- 1 cup Arborio rice
- 4 cups vegetable broth, warmed
- 1/2 cup walnuts, chopped and toasted
- 1/2 cup blue cheese, crumbled
- 1 onion, finely chopped
- 2 tbsp olive oil
- Salt and pepper, to taste

Directions:

1. In a large pan, heat olive oil over medium heat. Add onion and sauté until translucent.
2. Add Arborio rice and stir to coat in the oil.
3. Gradually add warm vegetable broth, one ladle at a time, stirring continuously. Allow each addition to be absorbed before adding the next.
4. Once the rice is creamy and al dente, remove from heat. Stir in toasted walnuts and crumbled blue cheese. Season with salt and pepper.
5. Serve immediately, garnished with extra walnuts if desired.

13. Caprese Pasta Salad

- Preparation Time: 10 minutes
- Cooking Time: 10 minutes
- Servings: 4

Ingredients:

- 12 oz whole wheat rotini
- 2 cups cherry tomatoes, halved
- 1 cup mozzarella balls, halved
- 1/4 cup fresh basil, chopped
- 1/4 cup balsamic reduction
- 2 tbsp olive oil
- Salt and pepper, to taste

Directions:

1. Cook rotini according to package instructions until al dente.
2. Drain and rinse under cold water to cool.
3. In a large bowl, combine cooled pasta with cherry tomatoes, mozzarella balls, and fresh basil.
4. Drizzle with olive oil and balsamic reduction.
5. Season with salt and pepper and toss to combine.
6. Serve chilled or at room temperature.

14. Pumpkin and Sage Risotto

- Preparation Time: 15 minutes
- Cooking Time: 30 minutes
- Servings: 4

Ingredients:

- 1 cup Arborio rice
- 2 cups pumpkin, cubed
- 4 cups vegetable broth, warmed
- 1/4 cup Parmesan cheese, grated
- 1/4 cup fresh sage, chopped
- 1 onion, finely chopped
- 2 tbsp olive oil
- Salt and pepper, to taste

Directions:

1. In a large pan, heat olive oil over medium heat. Add onion and sauté until translucent.
2. Add pumpkin cubes and cook until they begin to soften.
3. Add Arborio rice and stir to coat with the pumpkin and onion mixture.
4. Gradually add warm vegetable broth, one ladle at a time, stirring continuously. Allow each addition to be absorbed before adding the next.
5. Once the rice is creamy and al dente, remove from heat. Stir in Parmesan cheese and fresh sage. Season with salt and pepper.
6. Serve immediately, garnished with extra sage if desired.

15. Roasted Red Pepper Pasta

- Preparation Time: 10 minutes
- Cooking Time: 20 minutes
- Servings: 4

Ingredients:

- 12 oz whole wheat spaghetti
- 2 red bell peppers, roasted and peeled
- 1/4 cup sundried tomatoes, chopped
- 1/4 cup goat cheese, crumbled
- 2 cloves garlic, minced
- 2 tbsp olive oil
- Salt and pepper, to taste
- Fresh basil, for garnish

Directions:

1. Cook spaghetti according to package instructions until al dente.
2. While pasta cooks, blend roasted red peppers and sundried tomatoes in a blender until smooth.
3. Heat olive oil in a large skillet over medium heat. Add garlic and sauté until fragrant.
4. Pour the red pepper sauce into the skillet and heat through.
5. Drain pasta and add to the skillet, tossing to coat with the sauce.
6. Crumble goat cheese over the pasta.
7. Season with salt and pepper.
8. Garnish with fresh basil and serve.

16. Garlic and Oil Spaghetti (Aglio e Olio)

- Preparation Time: 5 minutes
- Cooking Time: 10 minutes
- Servings: 4

Ingredients:

- 12 oz spaghetti, whole wheat
- 4 cloves garlic, sliced
- 1/2 tsp red pepper flakes
- 1/4 cup extra-virgin olive oil
- Salt and pepper, to taste
- Fresh parsley, chopped for garnish

Directions:

1. Cook spaghetti according to package instructions until al dente.
2. While pasta cooks, heat olive oil in a large skillet over medium heat. Add garlic and red pepper flakes. Cook until garlic is golden.
3. Drain pasta and add to the skillet, tossing to coat with the garlic oil.
4. Season with salt and pepper.
5. Garnish with chopped parsley and serve immediately.

17. Broccoli and Anchovy Pasta

- Preparation Time: 10 minutes
- Cooking Time: 15 minutes
- Servings: 4

Ingredients:

- 12 oz orecchiette pasta
- 1 broccoli head, cut into florets
- 4 anchovy fillets, minced
- 2 cloves garlic, minced
- 1/4 cup extra-virgin olive oil
- 1/4 tsp red pepper flakes

- Salt and pepper, to taste

Directions:

1. Cook orecchiette according to package instructions until al dente.
2. In the last 5 minutes of cooking, add broccoli florets to the pasta water.
3. While pasta and broccoli cook, heat olive oil in a large skillet over medium heat. Add anchovies, garlic, and red pepper flakes. Cook until anchovies dissolve.
4. Drain pasta and broccoli and add to the skillet, tossing to coat with the anchovy mixture.
5. Season with salt and pepper.
6. Serve immediately.

Nutritious Legumes and Beans

1. Chickpea Salad

- Preparation Time: 15 minutes
- Cooking Time: 0 minutes
- Servings: 4

Ingredients:

- 1 can (15 oz) chickpeas, rinsed and drained
- 1 cucumber, diced
- 1 bell pepper, diced
- 1/2 red onion, finely chopped
- 1/4 cup parsley, chopped
- Juice of 1 lemon
- 3 tbsp olive oil
- Salt and pepper, to taste
- 1/4 cup feta cheese, crumbled (optional)

Directions:

1. In a large bowl, combine chickpeas, cucumber, bell pepper, red onion, and parsley.
2. In a small bowl, whisk together lemon juice, olive oil, salt, and pepper.
3. Pour the dressing over the salad and toss to combine.
4. Sprinkle feta cheese on top before serving.

2. Lentil Soup

- Preparation Time: 10 minutes
- Cooking Time: 40 minutes
- Servings: 6

Ingredients:

- 1 cup dried lentils, rinsed
- 1 onion, chopped
- 2 carrots, diced
- 2 celery stalks, diced
- 3 cloves garlic, minced
- 1 can (14.5 oz) diced tomatoes
- 6 cups vegetable broth
- 2 tsp cumin
- 2 tbsp olive oil
- Salt and pepper, to taste
- Fresh parsley, for garnish

Directions:

1. Heat olive oil in a large pot over medium heat.
2. Add onions, carrots, and celery, and sauté until softened.
3. Stir in garlic and cumin and cook for another minute.
4. Add lentils, diced tomatoes, and vegetable broth.
5. Bring to a boil, then reduce heat and simmer for 30-35 minutes, until lentils are tender.
6. Season with salt and pepper.
7. Garnish with fresh parsley before serving.

3. White Bean and Kale Stew

- Preparation Time: 15 minutes
- Cooking Time: 25 minutes
- Servings: 4

Ingredients:

- 1 can (15 oz) white beans, rinsed and drained
- 1 bunch kale, stems removed and leaves chopped
- 1 onion, chopped
- 2 cloves garlic, minced
- 1 carrot, diced
- 4 cups vegetable broth
- 2 tbsp olive oil
- 1 tsp smoked paprika
- Salt and pepper, to taste
- Lemon wedges, for serving

Directions:

1. Heat olive oil in a large pot over medium heat.
2. Add onion and carrot, and cook until softened.
3. Add garlic and smoked paprika, cooking for another minute until fragrant.
4. Stir in kale and cook until it begins to wilt.
5. Add white beans and vegetable broth.
6. Bring to a boil, then reduce heat and simmer for 15 minutes.
7. Season with salt and pepper.
8. Serve hot with a squeeze of lemon.

4. Mediterranean Black Bean Salad

- Preparation Time: 15 minutes
- Cooking Time: 0 minutes
- Servings: 4

Ingredients:

- 1 can (15 oz) black beans, rinsed and drained
- 1 red bell pepper, diced
- 1/2 red onion, finely chopped
- 1/4 cup cilantro, chopped
- Juice of 1 lime
- 3 tbsp olive oil
- Salt and pepper, to taste
- 1 avocado, diced

Directions:

1. In a large bowl, combine black beans, red bell pepper, red onion, and cilantro.
2. In a small bowl, whisk together lime juice, olive oil, salt, and pepper.
3. Pour the dressing over the bean mixture and toss to combine.
4. Gently fold in avocado just before serving.

5. Tuscan White Bean Pasta

- Preparation Time: 10 minutes
- Cooking Time: 20 minutes
- Servings: 4

Ingredients:

- 8 oz whole wheat pasta
- 1 can (15 oz) white beans, rinsed and drained
- 1 can (14.5 oz) diced tomatoes
- 1 onion, chopped
- 3 cloves garlic, minced
- 1/4 cup basil, chopped
- 2 tbsp olive oil
- Salt and pepper, to taste
- Grated Parmesan cheese, for serving

Directions:

1. Cook pasta according to package instructions until al dente. Drain and set aside.
2. Heat olive oil in a large skillet over medium heat.
3. Add onion and garlic, sautéing until the onion is translucent.
4. Stir in tomatoes and cook for 5 minutes.
5. Add white beans and cooked pasta, tossing to combine.
6. Cook for an additional 5 minutes to heat through.

7. Stir in basil and season with salt and pepper.

8. Serve with grated Parmesan cheese sprinkled on top.

6. Spiced Chickpea Wraps

- Preparation Time: 15 minutes
- Cooking Time: 10 minutes
- Servings: 4

Ingredients:

- 1 can (15 oz) chickpeas, rinsed and drained
- 1 tsp cumin
- 1 tsp paprika
- 1/2 tsp chili powder
- 4 whole wheat tortillas
- 1/2 cup tzatziki sauce
- 1/2 red onion, thinly sliced
- 1/4 cup fresh mint, chopped
- 2 tbsp olive oil

Directions:

1. Heat olive oil in a skillet over medium heat.
2. Add chickpeas and spices, cooking until chickpeas are golden and crispy.
3. Warm tortillas in the microwave or on another skillet.
4. Spread tzatziki sauce on each tortilla.
5. Top with spiced chickpeas, red onion, and fresh mint.
6. Roll up the tortillas and serve.

7. Moroccan Lentil Salad

- Preparation Time: 10 minutes
- Cooking Time: 20 minutes
- Servings: 4

Ingredients:

- 1 cup green lentils
- 1 carrot, grated
- 1/2 red onion, finely chopped
- 1/4 cup dried apricots, chopped
- 1/4 cup almonds, chopped
- 1/4 cup parsley, chopped
- 3 tbsp olive oil
- Juice of 1 lemon
- 1 tsp cumin
- Salt and pepper, to taste

Directions:

1. Cook lentils in boiling water for 20 minutes or until tender. Drain and let cool.
2. In a large bowl, combine cooked lentils, carrot, red onion, dried apricots, almonds, and parsley.
3. In a small bowl, whisk together olive oil, lemon juice, cumin, salt, and pepper.
4. Pour dressing over the lentil mixture and toss to combine.
5. Serve chilled or at room temperature.

8. Bean and Spinach Tacos

- Preparation Time: 10 minutes
- Cooking Time: 10 minutes
- Servings: 4

Ingredients:

- 1 can (15 oz) pinto beans, rinsed and drained
- 1 tsp chili powder
- 1/2 tsp cumin
- 4 whole wheat tortillas
- 2 cups spinach, chopped
- 1/2 cup salsa
- 1/4 cup cheddar cheese, shredded
- 2 tbsp olive oil

Directions:

1. Heat olive oil in a skillet over medium heat.
2. Add beans, chili powder, and cumin, cooking until beans are heated through.
3. Warm tortillas in the microwave or on another skillet.
4. Place a scoop of bean mixture onto each tortilla.
5. Top with spinach, salsa, and cheddar cheese.
6. Fold tortillas and serve.

9. Mediterranean Lentil Stew

- Preparation Time: 15 minutes
- Cooking Time: 35 minutes
- Servings: 6

Ingredients:

- 1 cup brown lentils, rinsed
- 1 onion, chopped
- 2 carrots, diced
- 2 celery stalks, diced
- 3 cloves garlic, minced
- 1 can (14.5 oz) diced tomatoes
- 6 cups vegetable broth

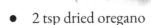

- 2 tsp dried oregano
- 2 tbsp olive oil
- Salt and pepper, to taste
- Fresh parsley, for garnish

Directions:

1. Heat olive oil in a large pot over medium heat.
2. Add onions, carrots, and celery, and sauté until softened.
3. Stir in garlic and oregano and cook for another minute.
4. Add lentils, diced tomatoes, and vegetable broth.
5. Bring to a boil, then reduce heat and simmer for 30-35 minutes, until lentils are tender.
6. Season with salt and pepper.
7. Garnish with fresh parsley before serving.

10. Three-Bean Salad

- Preparation Time: 15 minutes
- Cooking Time: 0 minutes
- Servings: 4

Ingredients:

- 1 can (15 oz) kidney beans, rinsed and drained
- 1 can (15 oz) black beans, rinsed and drained
- 1 can (15 oz) chickpeas, rinsed and drained
- 1 red bell pepper, diced
- 1/2 red onion, finely chopped
- 1/4 cup cilantro, chopped
- 3 tbsp olive oil
- Juice of 1 lime
- Salt and pepper, to taste

Directions:

1. In a large bowl, combine all three types of beans, red bell pepper, red onion, and cilantro.
2. In a small bowl, whisk together olive oil, lime juice, salt, and pepper.
3. Pour the dressing over the bean mixture and toss to combine.
4. Serve chilled or at room temperature.

11. Hummus

- Preparation Time: 10 minutes
- Cooking Time: 0 minutes
- Servings: 4

Ingredients:

- 1 can (15 oz) chickpeas, rinsed and drained
- 2 tbsp tahini

- 2 cloves garlic, minced
- Juice of 1 lemon
- 3 tbsp olive oil
- Salt and pepper, to taste
- Paprika, for garnish

Directions:

1. In a food processor, combine chickpeas, tahini, garlic, lemon juice, and olive oil.
2. Blend until smooth, adding water as needed to achieve desired consistency.
3. Season with salt and pepper.
4. Transfer to a serving dish and sprinkle with paprika.
5. Serve with fresh vegetables or pita bread.

12. Italian White Bean Soup

- Preparation Time: 15 minutes
- Cooking Time: 30 minutes
- Servings: 6

Ingredients:

- 1 can (15 oz) white beans, rinsed and drained
- 1 onion, chopped
- 2 carrots, diced
- 2 celery stalks, diced
- 3 cloves garlic, minced
- 1 can (14.5 oz) diced tomatoes
- 6 cups vegetable broth
- 2 tsp dried basil
- 2 tbsp olive oil
- Salt and pepper, to taste
- Fresh basil, for garnish

Directions:

1. Heat olive oil in a large pot over medium heat.
2. Add onions, carrots, and celery, and sauté until softened.
3. Stir in garlic and dried basil and cook for another minute.
4. Add white beans, diced tomatoes, and vegetable broth.
5. Bring to a boil, then reduce heat and simmer for 25-30 minutes.
6. Season with salt and pepper.
7. Garnish with fresh basil before serving.

13. Baked Falafel

- Preparation Time: 20 minutes (plus soaking time for chickpeas)
- Cooking Time: 30 minutes
- Servings: 4

Ingredients:

- 1 cup dried chickpeas, soaked overnight and drained
- 1 onion, chopped
- 2 cloves garlic, minced
- 1/4 cup parsley, chopped
- 1 tsp cumin
- 1/2 tsp coriander
- 1/2 tsp salt
- 1/4 tsp pepper
- 2 tbsp olive oil

Directions:

1. Preheat oven to 375°F (190°C).
2. In a food processor, combine soaked chickpeas, onion, garlic, parsley, cumin, coriander, salt, and pepper. Process until mixture is finely ground.
3. Form mixture into small patties or balls.
4. Place falafel on a baking sheet greased with olive oil.
5. Bake for 25-30 minutes, turning halfway through, until golden and crispy.
6. Serve with tzatziki sauce or wrapped in pita bread with vegetables.

14. Smoky Black Bean Chili

- Preparation Time: 15 minutes
- Cooking Time: 30 minutes
- Servings: 6

Ingredients:

- 2 cans (15 oz each) black beans, rinsed and drained
- 1 onion, chopped
- 2 cloves garlic, minced
- 1 red bell pepper, chopped
- 1 can (14.5 oz) diced tomatoes
- 2 tbsp tomato paste
- 2 tsp smoked paprika
- 1 tsp cumin
- 1/2 tsp chili powder
- 3 cups vegetable broth
- 2 tbsp olive oil
- Salt and pepper, to taste

- Fresh cilantro, for garnish

Directions:

1. Heat olive oil in a large pot over medium heat.
2. Add onion, garlic, and bell pepper. Sauté until the onion is translucent.
3. Stir in smoked paprika, cumin, and chili powder, cooking for another minute until fragrant.
4. Add black beans, diced tomatoes, tomato paste, and vegetable broth.
5. Bring to a boil, then reduce heat and simmer for 25-30 minutes.
6. Season with salt and pepper.
7. Garnish with fresh cilantro before serving.

15. Spinach and Chickpea Curry

- Preparation Time: 10 minutes
- Cooking Time: 20 minutes
- Servings: 4

Ingredients:

- 1 can (15 oz) chickpeas, rinsed and drained
- 1 onion, chopped
- 2 cloves garlic, minced
- 1 tbsp ginger, grated
- 1 can (14.5 oz) diced tomatoes
- 4 cups spinach, fresh
- 1 tsp turmeric
- 1 tsp cumin
- 1/2 tsp chili powder
- 2 tbsp olive oil
- Salt and pepper, to taste

Directions:

1. Heat olive oil in a large skillet over medium heat.
2. Add onion and sauté until translucent.
3. Add garlic and ginger, cooking for another minute until fragrant.
4. Stir in turmeric, cumin, and chili powder.
5. Add chickpeas and diced tomatoes, cooking until the mixture starts to simmer.
6. Stir in spinach and cook until wilted.
7. Season with salt and pepper.
8. Serve hot, optionally over rice or with naan bread.

16. Red Lentil Patties

- Preparation Time: 15 minutes
- Cooking Time: 10 minutes
- Servings: 4

Ingredients:

- 1 cup red lentils, cooked and mashed
- 1 onion, finely chopped
- 2 cloves garlic, minced
- 1 carrot, grated
- 1/4 cup parsley, chopped
- 1 egg, beaten
- 1/2 cup breadcrumbs
- 1 tsp cumin
- Salt and pepper, to taste
- Olive oil for frying

Directions:

1. In a large bowl, combine mashed lentils, onion, garlic, carrot, parsley, egg, breadcrumbs, and cumin. Season with salt and pepper.
2. Form the mixture into patties.
3. Heat olive oil in a skillet over medium heat.
4. Fry patties for about 5 minutes on each side, or until golden and crispy.
5. Serve hot, with yogurt or your favorite dipping sauce.

17. Greek Fava Bean Dip

- Preparation Time: 10 minutes
- Cooking Time: 1 hour
- Servings: 4

Ingredients:

- 1 cup dried fava beans, rinsed
- 1 onion, quartered
- 2 cloves garlic, whole
- 3 tbsp olive oil
- Juice of 1 lemon
- Salt and pepper, to taste
- Olive oil and chopped parsley for garnish

Directions:

1. Place fava beans, onion, and garlic in a large pot and cover with water.
2. Bring to a boil, then reduce heat and simmer for about 1 hour, until beans are very soft.
3. Drain beans and remove onion and garlic.

4. In a food processor, combine cooked beans, olive oil, lemon juice, salt, and pepper. Blend until smooth.
5. Transfer to a serving dish and drizzle with additional olive oil and sprinkle with chopped parsley.
6. Serve with pita bread or vegetable sticks.

If you've found value and inspiration in the pages you've explored with me, I would be deeply grateful if you could take a moment to share your experience. Your feedback isn't just important for guiding other readers on their journey for knowledge and inspiration; it's also a crucial support for independent authors like me as we navigate our paths to growth and development.

Simply scanning the QR Code below will allow you to express your thoughts and insights:

Thank you for taking the time to support my work. Your opinion is incredibly valuable and contributes significantly to my growth and improvement.

Plant-Based Mediterranean Delights

1. Greek Stuffed Tomatoes (Gemista)

- Preparation Time: 20 minutes
- Cooking Time: 1 hour
- Servings: 4

Ingredients:
- 8 large tomatoes
- 1 cup cooked rice
- 1 onion, finely chopped
- 2 cloves garlic, minced
- 1/4 cup fresh parsley, chopped
- 1/4 cup fresh mint, chopped
- 1/4 cup olive oil
- Salt and pepper, to taste

Directions:
1. Preheat the oven to 375°F (190°C).
2. Cut the tops off the tomatoes and scoop out the insides, setting the pulp aside.
3. In a bowl, mix the rice, onion, garlic, parsley, mint, half of the olive oil, and the tomato pulp. Season with salt and pepper.
4. Stuff the tomatoes with the rice mixture and replace the tops.
5. Place the stuffed tomatoes in a baking dish, drizzle with the remaining olive oil, and bake for 1 hour, until the tomatoes are soft and the filling is hot.

2. Mediterranean Vegetable Paella

- Preparation Time: 15 minutes
- Cooking Time: 40 minutes
- Servings: 6

Ingredients:
- 1 cup Arborio rice
- 1 onion, chopped
- 2 bell peppers, sliced
- 1 zucchini, sliced
- 3 cloves garlic, minced
- 1/2 cup frozen peas
- 4 cups vegetable broth
- 1 tsp saffron threads
- 1/2 tsp smoked paprika
- 3 tbsp olive oil

- Salt and pepper, to taste
- Lemon wedges, for serving

Directions:

1. Heat olive oil in a large skillet over medium heat. Sauté onion, bell peppers, zucchini, and garlic until softened.
2. Add rice, saffron, and smoked paprika. Stir to coat the rice with the oil and spices.
3. Pour in the vegetable broth and bring to a boil. Reduce heat to low and simmer for 30 minutes.
4. Stir in peas and cook for an additional 10 minutes, until the rice is tender and the liquid is absorbed.
5. Season with salt and pepper. Serve with lemon wedges.

3. Falafel with Tahini Sauce

- Preparation Time: 20 minutes (plus soaking)
- Cooking Time: 10 minutes
- Servings: 4

Ingredients:

- 1 cup dried chickpeas, soaked overnight
- 1 onion, chopped
- 2 cloves garlic, minced
- 1/4 cup fresh parsley, chopped
- 1 tsp cumin
- 1 tsp coriander
- 1/2 tsp chili powder
- Salt to taste
- Oil for frying
- For the tahini sauce:
    - 1/4 cup tahini
    - 2 tbsp lemon juice
    - 1 clove garlic, minced
    - Water, as needed

Directions:

1. Drain and rinse the chickpeas. Process in a food processor with onion, garlic, parsley, cumin, coriander, chili powder, and salt until a coarse meal forms.
2. Shape the mixture into small balls or patties.
3. Heat oil in a deep fryer or skillet and fry the falafel until golden and crispy.
4. To make the tahini sauce, whisk together tahini, lemon juice, garlic, and enough water to achieve a pourable consistency.
5. Serve the falafel drizzled with tahini sauce.

4. Vegan Moussaka

- Preparation Time: 30 minutes
- Cooking Time: 1 hour
- Servings: 6

Ingredients:

- 2 eggplants, sliced
- 3 potatoes, sliced
- 1 onion, chopped
- 3 cloves garlic, minced
- 1 can (14 oz) crushed tomatoes
- 1/2 cup lentils, cooked
- 1 tsp cinnamon
- 1 tsp allspice
- 1/4 cup olive oil
- Salt and pepper, to taste
- For the béchamel:
    - 2 cups almond milk
    - 1/4 cup flour
    - 1/4 cup olive oil
    - Nutmeg, to taste

Directions:

1. Preheat the oven to 375°F (190°C).
2. Sauté onions and garlic in olive oil until translucent. Add crushed tomatoes, lentils, cinnamon, and allspice. Simmer for 20 minutes.
3. Fry or bake eggplant and potato slices until tender.
4. Layer eggplant, potatoes, and lentil mixture in a baking dish.
5. For the béchamel: Heat olive oil in a saucepan, whisk in flour until smooth. Gradually add almond milk, stirring continuously until thickened. Season with nutmeg.
6. Pour béchamel over the layers in the dish. Bake for 40 minutes, until golden.
7. Let cool slightly before serving.

5. Quinoa Tabbouleh

- Preparation Time: 15 minutes
- Cooking Time: 15 minutes
- Servings: 4

Ingredients:

- 1 cup quinoa, cooked
- 1 cucumber, diced
- 2 tomatoes, diced
- 1/4 cup fresh parsley, chopped

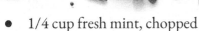

- 1/4 cup fresh mint, chopped
- Juice of 1 lemon
- 3 tbsp olive oil
- Salt and pepper, to taste

Directions:

1. In a large bowl, combine cooked quinoa, cucumber, tomatoes, parsley, and mint.
2. In a small bowl, whisk together lemon juice, olive oil, salt, and pepper.
3. Pour dressing over quinoa mixture and toss to combine.
4. Chill in the refrigerator before serving.

6. Spinach and Pine Nut Pasta

- Preparation Time: 10 minutes
- Cooking Time: 15 minutes
- Servings: 4

Ingredients:

- 12 oz whole wheat pasta
- 3 cups fresh spinach
- 1/4 cup pine nuts
- 3 cloves garlic, minced
- 1/4 cup olive oil
- Salt and pepper, to taste
- Lemon zest, for garnish

Directions:

1. Cook pasta according to package instructions. Drain and set aside.
2. In a large skillet, heat olive oil over medium heat. Add garlic and sauté until fragrant.
3. Add spinach and cook until wilted.
4. Toss cooked pasta with spinach, pine nuts, and additional olive oil if needed.
5. Season with salt, pepper, and lemon zest before serving.

7. Roasted Vegetable Couscous

- Preparation Time: 15 minutes
- Cooking Time: 30 minutes
- Servings: 4

Ingredients:

- 1 cup couscous, cooked
- 1 zucchini, cubed
- 1 bell pepper, cubed
- 1 red onion, cubed
- 2 carrots, cubed
- 1/4 cup olive oil

- 1 tsp cumin
- Salt and pepper, to taste
- Fresh cilantro, chopped for garnish

Directions:
1. Preheat oven to 400°F (200°C).
2. Toss vegetables with olive oil, cumin, salt, and pepper.
3. Roast in the oven for 30 minutes, stirring occasionally, until tender and browned.
4. Mix roasted vegetables with cooked couscous.
5. Garnish with fresh cilantro before serving.

8. Vegan Stuffed Peppers

- Preparation Time: 20 minutes
- Cooking Time: 1 hour
- Servings: 4

Ingredients:
- 4 bell peppers, tops cut off and seeds removed
- 1 cup brown rice, cooked
- 1 can (15 oz) black beans, rinsed and drained
- 1/2 cup corn kernels
- 1 onion, chopped
- 2 cloves garlic, minced
- 1 tsp chili powder
- 1/2 tsp cumin
- 1/4 cup tomato sauce
- 1/4 cup vegetable broth
- 2 tbsp olive oil
- Salt and pepper, to taste

Directions:
1. Preheat oven to 375°F (190°C).
2. Heat olive oil in a skillet over medium heat. Sauté onion and garlic until soft.
3. Add chili powder and cumin, cooking for another minute.
4. Stir in rice, black beans, corn, tomato sauce, and vegetable broth. Cook until everything is heated through.
5. Stuff the mixture into the bell peppers and place in a baking dish.
6. Cover with foil and bake for 50 minutes, until peppers are tender.
7. Remove foil and bake for an additional 10 minutes.
8. Serve warm.

9. Vegan Ratatouille

- Preparation Time: 20 minutes
- Cooking Time: 40 minutes
- Servings: 4

Ingredients:

- 1 eggplant, sliced
- 2 zucchinis, sliced
- 2 bell peppers, sliced
- 1 onion, sliced
- 3 tomatoes, sliced
- 3 cloves garlic, minced
- 1/4 cup olive oil
- 1 tbsp herbes de Provence
- Salt and pepper, to taste

Directions:

1. Preheat oven to 375°F (190°C).
2. Layer slices of eggplant, zucchini, bell peppers, onion, and tomatoes in a baking dish.
3. Sprinkle garlic, herbes de Provence, salt, and pepper between each layer.
4. Drizzle olive oil over the top.
5. Cover with foil and bake for 30 minutes.
6. Remove foil and bake for an additional 10 minutes, until vegetables are tender and lightly browned.
7. Serve hot or at room temperature.

10. Mediterranean Vegan Burger

- Preparation Time: 20 minutes
- Cooking Time: 10 minutes
- Servings: 4

Ingredients:

- 1 can (15 oz) chickpeas, drained and mashed
- 1/2 cup breadcrumbs
- 1/4 cup sun-dried tomatoes, chopped
- 1/4 cup olives, chopped
- 1/4 cup parsley, chopped
- 2 cloves garlic, minced
- 1 tsp cumin
- Salt and pepper, to taste
- Olive oil for frying

Directions:

1. In a bowl, mix together mashed chickpeas, breadcrumbs, sun-dried tomatoes, olives, parsley, garlic, cumin, salt, and pepper.
2. Form the mixture into patties.
3. Heat olive oil in a skillet over medium heat. Fry patties for about 5 minutes on each side, until crispy and golden.
4. Serve on burger buns with your choice of toppings.

11. Butternut Squash and Chickpea Stew

- Preparation Time: 20 minutes
- Cooking Time: 30 minutes
- Servings: 4

Ingredients:

- 1 butternut squash, peeled and cubed
- 1 can (15 oz) chickpeas, rinsed and drained
- 1 onion, chopped
- 2 cloves garlic, minced
- 1 tsp turmeric
- 1 tsp cumin
- 1/2 tsp cinnamon
- 4 cups vegetable broth
- 2 tbsp olive oil
- Salt and pepper, to taste
- Fresh cilantro, for garnish

Directions:

1. Heat olive oil in a large pot over medium heat. Sauté onion and garlic until soft.
2. Add turmeric, cumin, and cinnamon, cooking for another minute until fragrant.
3. Add butternut squash, chickpeas, and vegetable broth. Bring to a boil, then reduce heat and simmer for 25-30 minutes, until the squash is tender.
4. Season with salt and pepper.
5. Garnish with fresh cilantro before serving.

12. Mediterranean Lentil Meatballs

- Preparation Time: 30 minutes
- Cooking Time: 20 minutes
- Servings: 4

Ingredients:

- 1 cup lentils, cooked
- 1/2 cup breadcrumbs
- 1/4 cup sun-dried tomatoes, chopped

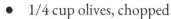

- 1/4 cup olives, chopped
- 1 onion, finely chopped
- 2 cloves garlic, minced
- 1 tsp oregano
- Salt and pepper, to taste
- Olive oil for baking

Directions:

1. Preheat oven to 375°F (190°C).
2. In a food processor, blend cooked lentils, breadcrumbs, sun-dried tomatoes, olives, onion, garlic, and oregano until combined. Season with salt and pepper.
3. Form the mixture into small balls and place on a baking sheet.
4. Drizzle with olive oil and bake for 20 minutes, until firm and golden.
5. Serve with marinara sauce or your favorite pasta.

13. Grilled Vegetable and Hummus Wrap

- Preparation Time: 15 minutes
- Cooking Time: 10 minutes
- Servings: 4

Ingredients:

- 4 whole wheat tortillas
- 1 zucchini, sliced and grilled
- 1 bell pepper, sliced and grilled
- 1/2 red onion, sliced and grilled
- 1 cup hummus
- 1/4 cup tahini sauce
- Fresh mint, chopped for garnish

Directions:

1. Spread hummus on each tortilla.
2. Top with grilled zucchini, bell pepper, and red onion.
3. Drizzle with tahini sauce and sprinkle with fresh mint.
4. Roll up the tortillas and serve.

14. Eggplant and Tomato Bake

- Preparation Time: 20 minutes
- Cooking Time: 40 minutes
- Servings: 4

Ingredients:

- 2 eggplants, sliced
- 4 tomatoes, sliced
- 3 cloves garlic, minced

- 1/4 cup fresh basil, chopped
- 1/4 cup olive oil
- Salt and pepper, to taste

Directions:

1. Preheat oven to 375°F (190°C).
2. Layer slices of eggplant and tomato in a baking dish, sprinkling garlic and basil between layers.
3. Drizzle with olive oil and season with salt and pepper.
4. Bake for 40 minutes, until vegetables are tender and lightly browned.
5. Serve warm.

15. Vegan Ceviche

- Preparation Time: 20 minutes
- Cooking Time: 0 minutes
- Servings: 4

Ingredients:

- 1 cup hearts of palm, chopped
- 1 avocado, diced
- 1 cucumber, diced
- 1/2 red onion, finely chopped
- Juice of 2 limes
- 1/4 cup cilantro, chopped
- 1 jalapeño, minced (optional)
- Salt and pepper, to taste

Directions:

1. In a bowl, combine hearts of palm, avocado, cucumber, red onion, lime juice, cilantro, and jalapeño if using.
2. Season with salt and pepper.
3. Chill in the refrigerator for at least 30 minutes before serving.

16. Stuffed Zucchini Boats

- Preparation Time: 20 minutes
- Cooking Time: 25 minutes
- Servings: 4

Ingredients:

- 4 zucchinis, halved lengthwise and scooped out
- 1 cup quinoa, cooked
- 1/2 cup black olives, chopped
- 1/2 cup sun-dried tomatoes, chopped
- 1/4 cup pine nuts
- 2 tbsp olive oil

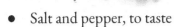

- Salt and pepper, to taste
- Fresh parsley, for garnish

Directions:

1. Preheat oven to 375°F (190°C).
2. Mix quinoa, olives, sun-dried tomatoes, and pine nuts in a bowl. Season with salt and pepper.
3. Stuff the zucchini halves with the quinoa mixture and place in a baking dish.
4. Drizzle with olive oil.
5. Bake for 25 minutes, until zucchini is tender.
6. Garnish with fresh parsley before serving.

17. Vegan Greek Salad

- Preparation Time: 15 minutes
- Cooking Time: 0 minutes
- Servings: 4

Ingredients:

- 3 tomatoes, chopped
- 1 cucumber, chopped
- 1 red onion, sliced
- 1/2 cup Kalamata olives
- 1/4 cup capers
- 1/4 cup olive oil
- Juice of 1 lemon
- Salt and pepper, to taste
- Fresh oregano, for garnish

Directions:

1. In a large bowl, combine tomatoes, cucumber, red onion, olives, and capers.
2. Whisk together olive oil, lemon juice, salt, and pepper.
3. Pour dressing over the salad and toss to coat.
4. Garnish with fresh oregano before serving.

Lean Meat and Poultry Creations

1. Greek Lemon Chicken

- Preparation Time: 10 minutes
- Cooking Time: 40 minutes
- Servings: 4

Ingredients:

- 4 boneless, skinless chicken breasts
- Juice of 2 lemons
- 4 cloves garlic, minced
- 2 tbsp olive oil
- 1 tbsp dried oregano
- Salt and pepper, to taste

Directions:

1. Preheat the oven to 375°F (190°C).
2. In a bowl, mix lemon juice, olive oil, garlic, oregano, salt, and pepper.
3. Place chicken breasts in a baking dish and pour the lemon marinade over them.
4. Bake for 35-40 minutes, or until the chicken is thoroughly cooked.
5. Serve with a side of roasted vegetables.

2. Turkish Beef Kebabs

- Preparation Time: 20 minutes (plus marinating)
- Cooking Time: 10 minutes
- Servings: 4

Ingredients:

- 1 lb lean beef, cut into cubes
- 1/4 cup yogurt
- 2 cloves garlic, minced
- 1 tsp paprika
- 1 tsp cumin
- 1/2 tsp coriander
- Salt and pepper, to taste
- Wooden or metal skewers

Directions:

1. In a bowl, mix yogurt, garlic, paprika, cumin, coriander, salt, and pepper.
2. Add beef cubes to the marinade and stir to coat. Refrigerate for at least 2 hours.
3. Thread beef onto skewers.
4. Preheat a grill or grill pan over medium-high heat. Cook skewers for about 4-5 minutes per side, or until the beef is cooked to your preference.

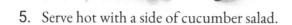

5. Serve hot with a side of cucumber salad.

3. Herb-Crusted Pork Tenderloin

- Preparation Time: 15 minutes
- Cooking Time: 30 minutes
- Servings: 4

Ingredients:

- 1 pork tenderloin (about 1 lb)
- 1 tbsp olive oil
- 2 cloves garlic, minced
- 1 tbsp rosemary, minced
- 1 tbsp thyme, minced
- Salt and pepper, to taste

Directions:

1. Preheat the oven to 375°F (190°C).
2. Rub the pork tenderloin with olive oil, then coat with minced garlic, rosemary, thyme, salt, and pepper.
3. Place the pork in a roasting pan and cook in the oven for about 25-30 minutes, or until the internal temperature reaches 145°F (63°C).
4. Let the pork rest for 5 minutes before slicing. Serve with steamed green beans.

4. Mediterranean Turkey Burgers

- Preparation Time: 15 minutes
- Cooking Time: 10 minutes
- Servings: 4

Ingredients:

- 1 lb ground turkey
- 1/4 cup finely chopped red onion
- 1/4 cup chopped fresh parsley
- 2 cloves garlic, minced
- 1 tsp cumin
- 1 tsp smoked paprika
- Salt and pepper, to taste
- Whole wheat burger buns

Directions:

1. In a bowl, combine ground turkey, red onion, parsley, garlic, cumin, smoked paprika, salt, and pepper.
2. Form the mixture into 4 burger patties.
3. Grill the patties over medium heat for about 5 minutes on each side, or until fully cooked.
4. Serve on whole wheat buns with lettuce, tomato, and a dollop of yogurt sauce.

5. Chicken and Artichoke Heart Skillet

- Preparation Time: 10 minutes
- Cooking Time: 20 minutes
- Servings: 4

Ingredients:

- 4 boneless, skinless chicken thighs
- 1 can artichoke hearts, drained and quartered
- 1 cup cherry tomatoes
- 1 onion, sliced
- 3 cloves garlic, minced
- 2 tbsp olive oil
- 1 lemon, juiced
- Salt and pepper, to taste
- Fresh parsley, chopped for garnish

Directions:

1. Heat olive oil in a large skillet over medium heat.
2. Add chicken thighs and cook until browned on both sides.
3. Add onion and garlic to the skillet and sauté until soft.
4. Stir in artichoke hearts, cherry tomatoes, and lemon juice. Season with salt and pepper.
5. Cook for an additional 10 minutes, until the chicken is fully cooked and the tomatoes are soft.
6. Garnish with fresh parsley before serving.

6. Baked Fish with Olives and Capers

- Preparation Time: 10 minutes
- Cooking Time: 20 minutes
- Servings: 4

Ingredients:

- 4 white fish fillets (such as cod or tilapia)
- 1/2 cup Kalamata olives, pitted and sliced
- 1/4 cup capers
- 2 tomatoes, sliced
- 1 lemon, sliced
- 2 tbsp olive oil
- Salt and pepper, to taste

Directions:

1. Preheat the oven to 375°F (190°C).
2. Place fish fillets in a baking dish. Top with olive slices, capers, tomato slices, and lemon slices. Drizzle with olive oil and season with salt and pepper.
3. Bake for 20 minutes, or until the fish flakes easily with a fork.
4. Serve hot, garnished with fresh herbs if desired.

7. Moroccan Spiced Lamb Stew

- Preparation Time: 20 minutes
- Cooking Time: 1 hour 30 minutes
- Servings: 4

Ingredients:

- 1 lb lamb shoulder, cut into cubes
- 1 onion, chopped
- 2 carrots, diced
- 1 can (14 oz) diced tomatoes
- 3 cups chicken or beef broth
- 2 tsp ground cumin
- 1 tsp ground coriander
- 1/2 tsp cinnamon
- 2 tbsp olive oil
- Salt and pepper, to taste
- Fresh cilantro, for garnish

Directions:

1. Heat olive oil in a large pot over medium heat. Add lamb cubes and brown on all sides.
2. Add onion and carrots to the pot and sauté until onions are translucent.
3. Stir in diced tomatoes, broth, cumin, coriander, and cinnamon. Season with salt and pepper.
4. Bring to a boil, then reduce heat and simmer, covered, for about 1 hour and 30 minutes, until the lamb is tender.
5. Garnish with fresh cilantro before serving.

8. Italian Herb Chicken

- Preparation Time: 10 minutes
- Cooking Time: 25 minutes
- Servings: 4

Ingredients:

- 4 boneless, skinless chicken breasts
- 2 tbsp olive oil
- 1 tbsp Italian seasoning
- 2 cloves garlic, minced

- Salt and pepper, to taste
- Fresh basil, for garnish

Directions:

1. Preheat the oven to 375°F (190°C).
2. Rub chicken breasts with olive oil and season with Italian seasoning, garlic, salt, and pepper.
3. Place chicken in a baking dish and bake for 25 minutes, or until the chicken is cooked through.
4. Garnish with fresh basil leaves before serving.

9. Lemon Herb Roasted Turkey

- Preparation Time: 20 minutes
- Cooking Time: 2 hours
- Servings: 6

Ingredients:

- 1 whole turkey breast (about 3-4 lbs)
- 1 lemon, sliced
- 4 cloves garlic, minced
- 2 tbsp olive oil
- 1 tbsp dried rosemary
- 1 tbsp dried thyme
- Salt and pepper, to taste

Directions:

1. Preheat the oven to 350°F (175°C).
2. Place turkey breast in a roasting pan. Rub with olive oil, garlic, rosemary, thyme, salt, and pepper.
3. Place lemon slices on and around the turkey.
4. Roast in the oven for about 2 hours, or until the internal temperature reaches 165°F (74°C).
5. Let rest before slicing. Serve garnished with additional herbs and lemon slices.

10. Grilled Tuna Steaks

- Preparation Time: 10 minutes
- Cooking Time: 10 minutes
- Servings: 4

Ingredients:

- 4 tuna steaks
- 2 tbsp olive oil
- 1 tbsp lemon juice
- 2 cloves garlic, minced
- Salt and pepper, to taste

Directions:

1. Preheat grill to high heat.

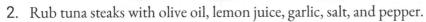

2. Rub tuna steaks with olive oil, lemon juice, garlic, salt, and pepper.
3. Grill steaks for about 5 minutes on each side, or until desired doneness is reached.
4. Serve immediately with a side of mixed greens.

11. Spanish Chicken and Rice

- Preparation Time: 15 minutes
- Cooking Time: 40 minutes
- Servings: 4

Ingredients:

- 4 chicken thighs, bone-in and skin-on
- 1 cup long-grain rice
- 1 onion, chopped
- 1 bell pepper, chopped
- 2 cloves garlic, minced
- 1/2 cup diced tomatoes
- 2 cups chicken broth
- 1 tsp paprika
- 1/2 tsp saffron threads
- 2 tbsp olive oil
- Salt and pepper, to taste

Directions:

1. Heat olive oil in a large skillet over medium heat. Add chicken thighs and brown on both sides.
2. Remove chicken and set aside. In the same skillet, add onion, bell pepper, and garlic. Sauté until softened.
3. Stir in rice, diced tomatoes, chicken broth, paprika, and saffron. Season with salt and pepper.
4. Return chicken to the skillet, cover, and simmer for 30 minutes, or until the rice is cooked and the chicken is done.
5. Serve hot, garnished with fresh herbs.

12. Beef and Vegetable Stir-Fry

- Preparation Time: 15 minutes
- Cooking Time: 10 minutes
- Servings: 4

Ingredients:

- 1 lb lean beef strips
- 1 bell pepper, sliced
- 1 onion, sliced
- 2 cups broccoli florets
- 2 cloves garlic, minced
- 2 tbsp soy sauce

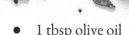

- 1 tbsp olive oil
- Salt and pepper, to taste

Directions:

1. Heat olive oil in a large skillet or wok over high heat.
2. Add beef strips and stir-fry until they start to brown.
3. Add bell pepper, onion, broccoli, and garlic. Continue to stir-fry until vegetables are tender-crisp.
4. Stir in soy sauce and cook for an additional minute.
5. Season with salt and pepper. Serve hot.

13. Rosemary Garlic Lamb Chops

- Preparation Time: 10 minutes (plus marinating)
- Cooking Time: 10 minutes
- Servings: 4

Ingredients:

- 8 lamb chops
- 1/4 cup olive oil
- 2 tbsp fresh rosemary, chopped
- 4 cloves garlic, minced
- Salt and pepper, to taste

Directions:

1. In a bowl, mix olive oil, rosemary, garlic, salt, and pepper.
2. Coat lamb chops with the marinade and let sit for at least 30 minutes.
3. Preheat grill or grill pan to medium-high heat.
4. Grill lamb chops for about 5 minutes on each side, or until they reach desired doneness.
5. Serve immediately, garnished with additional rosemary if desired.

14. Parmesan Crusted Chicken

- Preparation Time: 10 minutes
- Cooking Time: 20 minutes
- Servings: 4

Ingredients:

- 4 boneless, skinless chicken breasts
- 1/2 cup grated Parmesan cheese
- 1/4 cup whole wheat breadcrumbs
- 1 tsp dried Italian seasoning
- 2 tbsp olive oil
- Salt and pepper, to taste

Directions:

1. Preheat the oven to 400°F (200°C).

2. In a bowl, mix Parmesan cheese, breadcrumbs, Italian seasoning, salt, and pepper.
3. Brush chicken breasts with olive oil and coat with the Parmesan mixture.
4. Place chicken in a baking dish and bake for 20 minutes, or until the chicken is cooked through and the crust is golden.
5. Serve hot, garnished with fresh basil leaves.

15. Honey Mustard Turkey Cutlets

- Preparation Time: 10 minutes
- Cooking Time: 10 minutes
- Servings: 4

Ingredients:
- 4 turkey cutlets
- 2 tbsp honey
- 2 tbsp mustard
- 2 tbsp olive oil
- Salt and pepper, to taste

Directions:
1. In a small bowl, mix honey, mustard, and olive oil.
2. Season turkey cutlets with salt and pepper.
3. Heat a skillet over medium-high heat and cook the turkey cutlets for about 5 minutes on each side, or until cooked through.
4. In the last few minutes of cooking, brush the honey mustard sauce over the turkey cutlets.
5. Serve hot with a side of steamed vegetables.

16. Roast Chicken with Vegetables

- Preparation Time: 20 minutes
- Cooking Time: 1 hour 20 minutes
- Servings: 4

Ingredients:
- 1 whole chicken (about 4 lbs)
- 1 lemon, halved
- 4 cloves garlic, minced
- 1 onion, quartered
- 2 carrots, sliced
- 2 potatoes, cubed
- 1/4 cup olive oil
- 1 tbsp dried thyme
- Salt and pepper, to taste

Directions:
1. Preheat the oven to 425°F (220°C).

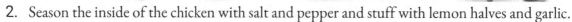

2. Season the inside of the chicken with salt and pepper and stuff with lemon halves and garlic.
3. Toss the vegetables with olive oil, thyme, salt, and pepper. Place them in a roasting pan.
4. Place the chicken on top of the vegetables. Roast for about 1 hour and 20 minutes, or until the chicken's internal temperature reaches 165°F (74°C) and the vegetables are tender.
5. Let the chicken rest before carving. Serve with roasted vegetables.

17. Beef Stroganoff

- Preparation Time: 15 minutes
- Cooking Time: 20 minutes
- Servings: 4

Ingredients:

- 1 lb lean beef strips
- 1 onion, chopped
- 2 cups mushrooms, sliced
- 1 cup beef broth
- 1/2 cup Greek yogurt
- 2 tbsp olive oil
- 1 tbsp whole wheat flour
- Salt and pepper, to taste
- Fresh parsley, for garnish

Directions:

1. Heat olive oil in a large skillet over medium heat. Add beef strips and brown on all sides. Remove from the skillet and set aside.
2. In the same skillet, add onion and mushrooms. Cook until softened.
3. Sprinkle flour over the mushrooms and onions, stir to coat.
4. Slowly pour in beef broth, stirring continuously. Bring to a simmer.
5. Return the beef to the skillet, reduce heat, and simmer for 10 minutes.
6. Stir in Greek yogurt and heat through, making sure not to boil.
7. Season with salt and pepper. Garnish with fresh parsley before serving.

Fresh and Flavorful Fish & Seafood

1. Grilled Salmon with Dill and Lemon

- Preparation Time: 10 minutes
- Cooking Time: 15 minutes
- Servings: 4

Ingredients:

- 4 salmon fillets
- 2 tbsp olive oil
- Juice of 1 lemon
- 2 tbsp fresh dill, chopped
- Salt and pepper, to taste

Directions:

1. Preheat the grill to medium-high heat.
2. Rub each salmon fillet with olive oil and season with salt and pepper.
3. Grill the salmon for about 6-7 minutes on each side, or until cooked through.
4. Squeeze lemon juice over the cooked salmon and garnish with fresh dill.
5. Serve immediately.

2. Baked Cod with Cherry Tomatoes and Olives

- Preparation Time: 10 minutes
- Cooking Time: 20 minutes
- Servings: 4

Ingredients:

- 4 cod fillets
- 1 cup cherry tomatoes, halved
- 1/2 cup Kalamata olives, pitted
- 3 cloves garlic, minced
- 2 tbsp olive oil
- Salt and pepper, to taste

Directions:

1. Preheat the oven to 400°F (200°C).
2. Place cod fillets in a baking dish and surround with cherry tomatoes and olives.
3. Drizzle with olive oil and sprinkle with minced garlic, salt, and pepper.
4. Bake in the preheated oven for about 20 minutes, until the fish flakes easily with a fork.
5. Serve hot.

3. Mediterranean Shrimp Skillet

- Preparation Time: 15 minutes
- Cooking Time: 10 minutes
- Servings: 4

Ingredients:

- 1 lb shrimp, peeled and deveined
- 1 bell pepper, sliced
- 1 onion, sliced
- 2 cloves garlic, minced
- 1/2 cup feta cheese, crumbled
- 1/4 cup fresh parsley, chopped
- 2 tbsp olive oil
- Salt and pepper, to taste

Directions:

1. Heat olive oil in a large skillet over medium heat.
2. Add garlic, bell pepper, and onion, sautéing until softened.
3. Add shrimp and cook for about 5 minutes, or until pink and cooked through.
4. Stir in feta cheese and parsley, and season with salt and pepper.
5. Serve hot, directly from the skillet.

4. Fish Tacos with Cabbage Slaw

- Preparation Time: 20 minutes
- Cooking Time: 10 minutes
- Servings: 4

Ingredients:

- 4 white fish fillets, such as tilapia
- 8 corn tortillas
- 2 cups cabbage, shredded
- 1/2 cup plain yogurt
- 2 tbsp lime juice
- 1 tsp chili powder
- 2 tbsp olive oil
- Salt and pepper, to taste

Directions:

1. In a small bowl, mix yogurt, lime juice, salt, and pepper to make the slaw dressing.
2. Toss the shredded cabbage in the dressing and set aside.
3. Season fish fillets with chili powder, salt, and pepper.
4. Heat olive oil in a skillet over medium heat and cook the fish for about 5 minutes on each side.
5. Warm tortillas in a dry skillet.
6. Assemble the tacos by placing fish in tortillas and topping with cabbage slaw.

7. Serve with lime wedges.

5. Seafood Paella

- Preparation Time: 30 minutes
- Cooking Time: 40 minutes
- Servings: 6

Ingredients:

- 1/2 lb shrimp, peeled and deveined
- 1/2 lb mussels, cleaned and debearded
- 1/2 lb clams, cleaned
- 1 cup Arborio rice
- 1 onion, chopped
- 1 bell pepper, chopped
- 3 cloves garlic, minced
- 1/2 cup tomato sauce
- 3 cups fish broth
- 1/2 tsp saffron threads
- 2 tbsp olive oil
- Salt and pepper, to taste
- Fresh parsley, for garnish

Directions:

1. Heat olive oil in a large skillet or paella pan over medium heat.
2. Add onion, bell pepper, and garlic, cooking until softened.
3. Stir in rice and tomato sauce, coating the rice well.
4. Pour in fish broth and sprinkle in saffron, salt, and pepper. Bring to a simmer.
5. Nestle shrimp, mussels, and clams into the rice. Cover and cook for 20-25 minutes until rice is tender and seafood is cooked.
6. Garnish with parsley and serve directly from the pan.

6. Grilled Tuna with Olive Tapenade

- Preparation Time: 15 minutes
- Cooking Time: 10 minutes
- Servings: 4

Ingredients:

- 4 tuna steaks
- 1/2 cup black olives, pitted and chopped
- 2 tbsp capers
- 2 cloves garlic, minced
- 1 lemon, juiced
- 3 tbsp olive oil

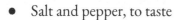

- Salt and pepper, to taste

Directions:

1. Preheat the grill to medium-high heat.
2. For the tapenade, mix olives, capers, garlic, lemon juice, and 1 tbsp olive oil in a small bowl.
3. Brush tuna steaks with the remaining olive oil and season with salt and pepper.
4. Grill the tuna for about 5 minutes on each side, or until desired doneness.
5. Top each steak with olive tapenade before serving.

7. Lemon Garlic Mussels

- Preparation Time: 10 minutes
- Cooking Time: 10 minutes
- Servings: 4

Ingredients:

- 2 lbs mussels, cleaned and debearded
- 4 cloves garlic, minced
- 1 lemon, juiced
- 1/4 cup white wine
- 2 tbsp olive oil
- Fresh parsley, chopped for garnish

Directions:

1. In a large pot, heat olive oil over medium heat.
2. Add garlic and cook until fragrant, about 1 minute.
3. Add white wine and lemon juice, bringing to a simmer.
4. Add mussels, cover the pot, and cook until all mussels have opened, about 7-8 minutes.
5. Discard any unopened mussels.
6. Garnish with parsley and serve with crusty bread to soak up the broth.

8. Spicy Grilled Shrimp

- Preparation Time: 15 minutes (plus marinating)
- Cooking Time: 10 minutes
- Servings: 4

Ingredients:

- 1 lb shrimp, peeled and deveined
- 2 tbsp olive oil
- 1 tsp chili powder
- 1/2 tsp paprika
- 1/4 tsp cayenne pepper
- Salt and pepper, to taste

Directions:

1. In a bowl, combine olive oil, chili powder, paprika, cayenne pepper, salt, and pepper.

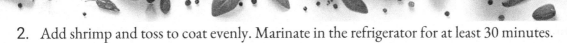

2. Add shrimp and toss to coat evenly. Marinate in the refrigerator for at least 30 minutes.
3. Preheat grill to high heat.
4. Grill shrimp for 2-3 minutes on each side or until opaque and slightly charred.
5. Serve immediately, garnished with lemon wedges.

9. Poached Fish in Tomato Basil Sauce

- Preparation Time: 10 minutes
- Cooking Time: 20 minutes
- Servings: 4

Ingredients:
- 4 white fish fillets, such as cod or tilapia
- 1 can (14 oz) diced tomatoes
- 1/4 cup fresh basil, chopped
- 2 cloves garlic, minced
- 2 tbsp olive oil
- Salt and pepper, to taste

Directions:
1. In a large skillet, heat olive oil over medium heat.
2. Add garlic and sauté until fragrant.
3. Stir in diced tomatoes and bring to a simmer.
4. Season fish fillets with salt and pepper, then nestle them into the tomato sauce.
5. Cover and cook for 10-15 minutes, or until fish is cooked through.
6. Sprinkle with fresh basil before serving.

10. Roasted Halibut with Fennel and Potatoes

- Preparation Time: 15 minutes
- Cooking Time: 25 minutes
- Servings: 4

Ingredients:
- 4 halibut fillets
- 2 fennel bulbs, thinly sliced
- 2 potatoes, thinly sliced
- 1 lemon, sliced
- 3 tbsp olive oil
- Salt and pepper, to taste

Directions:

1. Preheat the oven to 400°F (200°C).
2. In a large baking dish, layer sliced fennel and potatoes. Drizzle with 2 tbsp olive oil and season with salt and pepper.
3. Place halibut fillets on top of the fennel and potatoes. Top each fillet with a slice of lemon and drizzle with the remaining olive oil.
4. Roast in the preheated oven for 25 minutes, or until the fish is cooked through and the vegetables are tender.
5. Serve hot.

11. Seared Scallops with Lemon Butter Sauce

- Preparation Time: 10 minutes
- Cooking Time: 10 minutes
- Servings: 4

Ingredients:

- 12 large scallops
- 2 tbsp butter
- 1 lemon, juiced
- 2 tbsp olive oil
- Salt and pepper, to taste

Directions:

1. Heat olive oil in a large skillet over high heat.
2. Season scallops with salt and pepper. Place them in the skillet and sear for about 2 minutes on each side, until golden brown and slightly firm.
3. Remove scallops from the skillet and set aside.
4. Reduce heat to low and add butter and lemon juice to the skillet, whisking to combine into a sauce.
5. Return scallops to the skillet and coat with lemon butter sauce.
6. Serve immediately, garnished with fresh herbs if desired.

12. Clam Linguine

- Preparation Time: 10 minutes
- Cooking Time: 20 minutes
- Servings: 4

Ingredients:

- 1 lb linguine
- 2 lbs clams, cleaned
- 4 cloves garlic, minced
- 1/2 cup white wine
- 1/4 cup parsley, chopped

- 3 tbsp olive oil
- Salt and pepper, to taste

Directions:

1. Cook linguine according to package instructions until al dente. Drain and set aside.
2. In a large skillet, heat olive oil over medium heat. Add garlic and cook until fragrant.
3. Add clams and white wine. Cover and cook until clams have opened, about 7-8 minutes.
4. Toss cooked linguine with clams and the cooking liquid. Season with salt and pepper.
5. Garnish with chopped parsley before serving.

13. Mediterranean Octopus Salad

- Preparation Time: 20 minutes (plus cooking octopus)
- Cooking Time: 1 hour 30 minutes
- Servings: 4

Ingredients:

- 1 octopus, cleaned (about 2 lbs)
- 1 cucumber, diced
- 1 red onion, thinly sliced
- 1/2 cup Kalamata olives, pitted and sliced
- 1/4 cup fresh parsley, chopped
- Juice of 1 lemon
- 3 tbsp olive oil
- Salt and pepper, to taste

Directions:

1. Place the octopus in a pot and cover with water. Bring to a boil, then reduce heat and simmer for about 1.5 hours, until tender. Allow to cool in the liquid, then drain and cut into pieces.
2. In a large bowl, combine octopus, cucumber, red onion, olives, and parsley.
3. In a small bowl, whisk together lemon juice, olive oil, salt, and pepper.
4. Pour the dressing over the octopus salad and toss to combine.
5. Chill for at least 30 minutes before serving.

14. Sardines Grilled with Herbs

- Preparation Time: 10 minutes
- Cooking Time: 10 minutes
- Servings: 4

Ingredients:

- 12 fresh sardines, cleaned and gutted
- 1/4 cup fresh herbs (such as parsley, dill, and thyme), chopped
- 2 lemons, sliced
- 2 tbsp olive oil
- Salt and pepper, to taste

Directions:

1. Preheat grill to medium-high heat.
2. Rinse sardines and pat dry. Season inside and out with salt and pepper.
3. Stuff each sardine with herbs and a slice of lemon.
4. Brush the grill with olive oil and grill sardines for about 2-3 minutes on each side, until cooked through and crispy.
5. Serve immediately.

15. Simple Grilled Swordfish

- Preparation Time: 10 minutes
- Cooking Time: 12 minutes
- Servings: 4

Ingredients:

- 4 swordfish steaks
- 2 tbsp olive oil
- Salt and pepper, to taste
- Lemon wedges, for serving

Directions:

1. Preheat grill to high heat.
2. Brush swordfish steaks with olive oil and season with salt and pepper.
3. Grill steaks for about 6 minutes on each side, until cooked through and grill marks appear.
4. Serve hot with lemon wedges.

16. Smoked Trout Salad

- Preparation Time: 15 minutes
- Cooking Time: 0 minutes
- Servings: 4

Ingredients:

- 1 lb smoked trout, flaked
- 2 cups mixed salad greens
- 1 avocado, sliced
- 1/4 cup walnuts, chopped
- 1/4 cup dried cranberries
- 2 tbsp olive oil
- Juice of 1 lemon
- Salt and pepper, to taste

Directions:

1. In a large salad bowl, combine salad greens, flaked trout, avocado slices, walnuts, and dried cranberries.
2. In a small bowl, whisk together olive oil, lemon juice, salt, and pepper.
3. Drizzle the dressing over the salad and toss gently to combine.
4. Serve immediately.

17. Crab Stuffed Avocado

- Preparation Time: 15 minutes
- Cooking Time: 0 minutes
- Servings: 4

Ingredients:

- 2 avocados, halved and pitted
- 1 cup crab meat, cooked and shredded
- 1/4 cup mayonnaise
- 1 tbsp chives, chopped
- 1 tbsp cilantro, chopped
- 1 tsp lime juice
- Salt and pepper, to taste

Directions:

1. In a bowl, mix crab meat, mayonnaise, chives, cilantro, lime juice, salt, and pepper.
2. Spoon the crab mixture into the avocado halves.
3. Serve chilled as a refreshing and protein-rich appetizer.

Vibrant Mediterranean Salads

1. Classic Greek Salad

- Preparation Time: 15 minutes
- Cooking Time: 0 minutes
- Servings: 4

Ingredients:

- 3 tomatoes, cut into wedges
- 1 cucumber, sliced
- 1 red onion, thinly sliced
- 1/2 cup Kalamata olives
- 1/2 cup feta cheese, crumbled
- 3 tbsp olive oil
- 1 tbsp red wine vinegar
- Salt and pepper, to taste
- 1 tsp dried oregano

Directions:

1. In a large bowl, combine tomatoes, cucumber, red onion, and olives.
2. Drizzle with olive oil and red wine vinegar.
3. Season with salt, pepper, and oregano.
4. Sprinkle feta cheese over the top.
5. Toss gently to combine and serve immediately.

2. Tabbouleh

- Preparation Time: 20 minutes (plus resting)
- Cooking Time: 0 minutes
- Servings: 4

Ingredients:

- 1 cup bulgur wheat
- 1 1/2 cups boiling water
- 3 medium tomatoes, finely diced
- 1 cucumber, finely diced
- 4 green onions, chopped
- 1 cup fresh parsley, chopped
- 1/2 cup fresh mint, chopped
- 1/4 cup olive oil
- 1/4 cup lemon juice
- Salt and pepper, to taste

Directions:

1. Place bulgur in a large bowl and cover with boiling water. Let sit for about 30 minutes until water is absorbed and bulgur is tender.
2. Fluff the bulgur with a fork and let cool.
3. Add tomatoes, cucumber, green onions, parsley, and mint to the bulgur.
4. In a small bowl, whisk together olive oil and lemon juice. Season with salt and pepper.
5. Pour dressing over the salad and toss to combine.
6. Let the salad sit for at least 30 minutes to allow flavors to meld before serving.

3. Mediterranean Chickpea Salad

- Preparation Time: 15 minutes
- Cooking Time: 0 minutes
- Servings: 4

Ingredients:

- 1 can (15 oz) chickpeas, rinsed and drained
- 1 red bell pepper, diced
- 1/2 red onion, diced
- 1 cucumber, diced
- 1/4 cup fresh parsley, chopped
- 1/4 cup feta cheese, crumbled
- 3 tbsp olive oil
- 2 tbsp lemon juice
- Salt and pepper, to taste

Directions:

1. In a large bowl, combine chickpeas, bell pepper, red onion, cucumber, and parsley.
2. Drizzle with olive oil and lemon juice, and season with salt and pepper.
3. Toss to mix well.
4. Sprinkle with feta cheese just before serving.

4. Roasted Vegetable Salad

- Preparation Time: 15 minutes
- Cooking Time: 25 minutes
- Servings: 4

Ingredients:

- 2 bell peppers (different colors), cut into chunks
- 1 zucchini, sliced
- 1 eggplant, cubed
- 1 red onion, cut into wedges
- 1/4 cup olive oil
- Salt and pepper, to taste

- 2 tbsp balsamic vinegar
- 1/4 cup pine nuts, toasted

Directions:

1. Preheat the oven to 425°F (220°C).
2. Place bell peppers, zucchini, eggplant, and red onion on a baking sheet.
3. Drizzle with olive oil and season with salt and pepper. Toss to coat.
4. Roast in the preheated oven for about 25 minutes, or until vegetables are tender and caramelized.
5. Remove from the oven and drizzle with balsamic vinegar.
6. Sprinkle with toasted pine nuts before serving.

5. Watermelon and Feta Salad

- Preparation Time: 15 minutes
- Cooking Time: 0 minutes
- Servings: 4

Ingredients:

- 4 cups watermelon, cubed
- 1/2 cup feta cheese, crumbled
- 1/4 cup fresh mint, chopped
- 2 tbsp olive oil
- 1 tbsp balsamic reduction

Directions:

1. In a large bowl, combine watermelon, feta cheese, and fresh mint.
2. Drizzle with olive oil and balsamic reduction.
3. Gently toss to combine.
4. Serve chilled for a refreshing salad.

6. Beet and Goat Cheese Salad

- Preparation Time: 15 minutes
- Cooking Time: 1 hour (for roasting beets, if necessary)
- Servings: 4

Ingredients:

- 4 medium beets, roasted, peeled, and sliced
- 1/4 cup goat cheese, crumbled
- 1/4 cup walnuts, toasted and chopped
- 3 tbsp olive oil
- 1 tbsp red wine vinegar
- Salt and pepper, to taste
- Fresh arugula or mixed greens

Directions:

1. Arrange sliced beets over a bed of arugula or mixed greens.
2. Sprinkle with crumbled goat cheese and toasted walnuts.
3. In a small bowl, whisk together olive oil and red wine vinegar, and season with salt and pepper.
4. Drizzle the dressing over the salad before serving.

7. Cucumber and Yogurt Salad (Cacik)

- Preparation Time: 10 minutes
- Cooking Time: 0 minutes
- Servings: 4

Ingredients:

- 2 cucumbers, peeled and grated
- 2 cups Greek yogurt
- 2 cloves garlic, minced
- 2 tbsp fresh dill, chopped
- 1 tbsp olive oil
- Salt and pepper, to taste

Directions:

1. In a bowl, combine grated cucumber, Greek yogurt, minced garlic, and dill.
2. Drizzle with olive oil and season with salt and pepper.
3. Mix well and chill before serving.

8. Nicoise Salad

- Preparation Time: 20 minutes
- Cooking Time: 10 minutes (for eggs and potatoes)
- Servings: 4

Ingredients:

- 4 hard-boiled eggs, peeled and quartered
- 2 cups green beans, blanched
- 4 small potatoes, boiled and sliced
- 1/4 cup olives (preferably Niçoise)
- 2 cans (5 oz each) tuna, drained
- 1/4 cup olive oil
- 2 tbsp red wine vinegar
- Salt and pepper, to taste
- Mixed salad greens

Directions:

1. Arrange mixed salad greens on a large platter.
2. Top with sliced potatoes, green beans, olives, and chunks of tuna.
3. Place hard-boiled eggs around the salad.

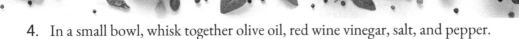

4. In a small bowl, whisk together olive oil, red wine vinegar, salt, and pepper.
5. Drizzle the dressing over the salad before serving.

9. Fattoush

- Preparation Time: 20 minutes
- Cooking Time: 10 minutes (for toasting bread)
- Servings: 4

Ingredients:

- 2 pita breads, toasted and broken into pieces
- 3 tomatoes, chopped
- 1 cucumber, chopped
- 1 bell pepper, chopped
- 1/2 red onion, thinly sliced
- 1/4 cup fresh mint, chopped
- 1/4 cup fresh parsley, chopped
- 1/4 cup olive oil
- 2 tbsp lemon juice
- Salt and sumac, to taste

Directions:

1. In a large bowl, combine tomatoes, cucumber, bell pepper, red onion, mint, and parsley.
2. Add toasted pita pieces.
3. In a small bowl, whisk together olive oil, lemon juice, salt, and sumac.
4. Pour dressing over the salad and toss to combine.
5. Serve immediately to maintain the crispness of the pita.

10. Spinach and Strawberry Salad

- Preparation Time: 10 minutes
- Cooking Time: 0 minutes
- Servings: 4

Ingredients:

- 4 cups fresh spinach leaves
- 1 cup strawberries, sliced
- 1/2 cup almonds, toasted and sliced
- 1/4 cup feta cheese, crumbled
- 3 tbsp olive oil
- 1 tbsp balsamic vinegar
- Salt and pepper, to taste

Directions:

1. In a large salad bowl, combine spinach, strawberries, and almonds.
2. Sprinkle with crumbled feta cheese.

3. In a small bowl, whisk together olive oil, balsamic vinegar, salt, and pepper.
4. Drizzle the dressing over the salad and toss gently to combine.
5. Serve immediately.

11. Carrot and Orange Salad

- Preparation Time: 15 minutes
- Cooking Time: 0 minutes
- Servings: 4

Ingredients:
- 4 large carrots, grated
- 2 oranges, peeled and segmented
- 1/4 cup raisins
- 2 tbsp olive oil
- 1 tbsp lemon juice
- 1 tsp ground cinnamon
- Salt, to taste

Directions:
1. In a large bowl, combine grated carrots, orange segments, and raisins.
2. In a small bowl, whisk together olive oil, lemon juice, cinnamon, and salt.
3. Pour the dressing over the carrot mixture and toss to coat evenly.
4. Chill in the refrigerator before serving.

12. Mediterranean Lentil Salad

- Preparation Time: 10 minutes
- Cooking Time: 25 minutes
- Servings: 4

Ingredients:
- 1 cup dried lentils
- 1 bell pepper, diced
- 1 cucumber, diced
- 1/2 red onion, diced
- 1/4 cup fresh parsley, chopped
- 1/4 cup olive oil
- 2 tbsp red wine vinegar
- Salt and pepper, to taste

1. Cook lentils according to package instructions until tender. Drain and let cool.
2. In a large bowl, combine cooled lentils, bell pepper, cucumber, red onion, and parsley.
3. In a small bowl, whisk together olive oil, red wine vinegar, salt, and pepper.
4. Pour the dressing over the lentil mixture and toss to combine.
5. Chill before serving.

13. Avocado and Tomato Salad

- Preparation Time: 10 minutes
- Cooking Time: 0 minutes
- Servings: 4

Ingredients:

- 2 avocados, diced
- 3 tomatoes, diced
- 1/4 cup red onion, finely chopped
- 1/4 cup cilantro, chopped
- 2 tbsp olive oil
- 1 lime, juiced
- Salt and pepper, to taste

Directions:

1. In a large bowl, combine avocados, tomatoes, red onion, and cilantro.
2. In a small bowl, whisk together olive oil, lime juice, salt, and pepper.
3. Pour the dressing over the avocado mixture and gently toss to combine.
4. Serve immediately to prevent the avocado from browning.

14. Broccoli and Chickpea Salad

- Preparation Time: 15 minutes
- Cooking Time: 0 minutes
- Servings: 4

Ingredients:

- 2 cups broccoli florets, blanched
- 1 can (15 oz) chickpeas, rinsed and drained
- 1/4 cup sun-dried tomatoes, chopped
- 1/4 cup almonds, toasted
- 2 tbsp olive oil
- 1 tbsp white wine vinegar
- Salt and pepper, to taste

Directions:

1. In a large bowl, combine broccoli, chickpeas, sun-dried tomatoes, and almonds.
2. In a small bowl, whisk together olive oil, white wine vinegar, salt, and pepper.

3. Pour the dressing over the broccoli mixture and toss to combine.
4. Serve chilled or at room temperature.

15. Quinoa and Vegetable Salad

- Preparation Time: 15 minutes
- Cooking Time: 15 minutes
- Servings: 4

Ingredients:

- 1 cup quinoa
- 2 cups water
- 1 cucumber, diced
- 1 bell pepper, diced
- 1/2 red onion, diced
- 1/4 cup fresh parsley, chopped
- 3 tbsp olive oil
- 2 tbsp lemon juice
- Salt and pepper, to taste

Directions:

1. Rinse quinoa under cold running water. In a saucepan, combine quinoa and water. Bring to a boil, reduce heat to low, cover, and simmer for 15 minutes or until water is absorbed.
2. Fluff quinoa with a fork and let cool.
3. In a large bowl, combine cooled quinoa, cucumber, bell pepper, red onion, and parsley.
4. In a small bowl, whisk together olive oil, lemon juice, salt, and pepper.
5. Pour the dressing over the quinoa mixture and toss to combine.
6. Chill in the refrigerator before serving.

16. Artichoke and Spinach Salad

- Preparation Time: 15 minutes
- Cooking Time: 0 minutes
- Servings: 4

Ingredients:

- 1 can (14 oz) artichoke hearts, drained and quartered
- 3 cups fresh spinach
- 1/4 cup parmesan cheese, shaved
- 1/4 cup pine nuts, toasted
- 3 tbsp olive oil
- 1 tbsp balsamic vinegar
- Salt and pepper, to taste

Directions:

1. In a large salad bowl, combine artichoke hearts, spinach, parmesan cheese, and pine nuts.

2. In a small bowl, whisk together olive oil, balsamic vinegar, salt, and pepper.
3. Drizzle the dressing over the salad and toss gently to combine.
4. Serve immediately.

17. Orange and Olive Salad

- Preparation Time: 15 minutes
- Cooking Time: 0 minutes
- Servings: 4

Ingredients:

- 3 oranges, peeled and sliced
- 1/2 cup black olives, pitted and sliced
- 1/4 red onion, thinly sliced
- 2 tbsp olive oil
- 1 tbsp white wine vinegar
- Salt and pepper, to taste
- Fresh mint, for garnish

Directions:

1. In a large salad bowl, arrange orange slices, black olives, and red onion.
2. In a small bowl, whisk together olive oil, white wine vinegar, salt, and pepper.
3. Pour the dressing over the salad and gently toss to combine.
4. Garnish with fresh mint leaves before serving.

Comforting Soups and Stews

1. Tuscan White Bean Soup

- Preparation Time: 10 minutes
- Cooking Time: 30 minutes
- Servings: 4

Ingredients:

- 2 cans (15 oz each) white beans, rinsed and drained
- 1 onion, chopped
- 2 carrots, diced
- 2 celery stalks, diced
- 4 cloves garlic, minced
- 4 cups vegetable broth
- 1 tsp dried thyme
- 2 tbsp olive oil
- Salt and pepper, to taste
- Fresh parsley, chopped for garnish

Directions:

1. Heat olive oil in a large pot over medium heat. Add onion, carrots, celery, and garlic. Sauté until vegetables are softened.
2. Add beans, vegetable broth, and thyme. Season with salt and pepper.
3. Bring to a boil, then reduce heat and simmer for about 20 minutes.
4. Puree part of the soup using an immersion blender for a creamy texture.
5. Serve hot, garnished with fresh parsley.

2. Moroccan Lentil Stew

- Preparation Time: 15 minutes
- Cooking Time: 45 minutes
- Servings: 6

Ingredients:

- 1 cup red lentils
- 1 sweet potato, cubed
- 1 onion, chopped
- 2 carrots, sliced
- 1 bell pepper, chopped
- 3 cloves garlic, minced
- 1 tsp ground cumin
- 1 tsp ground coriander
- 1/2 tsp ground cinnamon

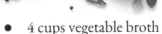

- 4 cups vegetable broth
- 1 can (14 oz) diced tomatoes
- 2 tbsp olive oil
- Salt and pepper, to taste
- Fresh cilantro, chopped for garnish

Directions:

1. Heat olive oil in a large pot over medium heat. Add onion, garlic, carrots, and bell pepper. Cook until softened.
2. Stir in cumin, coriander, and cinnamon, and cook for another minute.
3. Add lentils, sweet potato, diced tomatoes, and vegetable broth.
4. Bring to a boil, then reduce heat and simmer for about 30 minutes, or until lentils and sweet potatoes are tender.
5. Season with salt and pepper.
6. Serve hot, garnished with chopped cilantro.

3. Greek Lemon Chicken Soup

- Preparation Time: 10 minutes
- Cooking Time: 30 minutes
- Servings: 4

Ingredients:

- 4 cups chicken broth
- 2 chicken breasts, cooked and shredded
- 1/2 cup orzo pasta
- 3 eggs
- Juice of 2 lemons
- 1 onion, chopped
- 2 tbsp olive oil
- Salt and pepper, to taste

Directions:

1. Heat olive oil in a pot over medium heat. Add onion and cook until translucent.
2. Add chicken broth and bring to a boil.
3. Add orzo and cook until tender, about 10 minutes.
4. In a bowl, whisk together eggs and lemon juice.
5. Slowly ladle some hot broth into the egg mixture to temper it, then gradually stir the egg mixture into the pot.
6. Add shredded chicken, and heat through. Be careful not to let the soup boil to prevent the eggs from curdling.
7. Season with salt and pepper.
8. Serve hot.

4. Italian Minestrone

- Preparation Time: 15 minutes
- Cooking Time: 40 minutes
- Servings: 6

Ingredients:

- 1 onion, chopped
- 2 carrots, diced
- 2 celery stalks, diced
- 3 cloves garlic, minced
- 1 zucchini, diced
- 1 cup green beans, trimmed and cut into 1-inch pieces
- 1 can (15 oz) kidney beans, rinsed and drained
- 1 can (15 oz) diced tomatoes
- 4 cups vegetable broth
- 1/2 cup small pasta, such as ditalini
- 2 tbsp olive oil
- 1 tsp dried basil
- 1 tsp dried oregano
- Salt and pepper, to taste
- Parmesan cheese, grated, for serving

Directions:

1. Heat olive oil in a large pot over medium heat. Add onion, carrots, celery, and garlic. Sauté until vegetables begin to soften.
2. Add zucchini and green beans, cooking for another 5 minutes.
3. Stir in kidney beans, diced tomatoes, vegetable broth, basil, and oregano. Bring to a boil.
4. Reduce heat and simmer for 20 minutes.
5. Add pasta and cook until al dente, about 10 minutes.
6. Season with salt and pepper.
7. Serve hot, topped with grated Parmesan cheese.

5. Spanish Seafood Stew

- Preparation Time: 20 minutes
- Cooking Time: 30 minutes
- Servings: 4

Ingredients:

- 1 lb mixed seafood (shrimp, mussels, and clams)
- 1 onion, chopped
- 2 cloves garlic, minced
- 1 bell pepper, chopped
- 1 can (14 oz) diced tomatoes

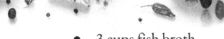

- 3 cups fish broth
- 1/2 cup white wine
- 1 tsp smoked paprika
- 2 tbsp olive oil
- Salt and pepper, to taste
- Fresh parsley, chopped for garnish

Directions:

1. Heat olive oil in a large pot over medium heat. Add onion, garlic, and bell pepper. Cook until vegetables are softened.
2. Stir in diced tomatoes, fish broth, white wine, and smoked papaprika. Bring to a simmer.
3. Add seafood and cook until mussels and clams open and shrimp is cooked through, about 10 minutes.
4. Season with salt and pepper.
5. Garnish with fresh parsley and serve hot.

6. French Onion Soup

- Preparation Time: 10 minutes
- Cooking Time: 50 minutes
- Servings: 4

Ingredients:

- 4 large onions, thinly sliced
- 4 cups beef broth
- 1/2 cup dry white wine
- 2 tbsp butter
- 1 tsp sugar
- Salt and pepper, to taste
- 4 slices of crusty bread
- 1/2 cup grated Gruyere cheese

Directions:

1. In a large pot, melt butter over medium heat. Add onions and sugar, cooking until onions are caramelized, about 30 minutes, stirring frequently.
2. Add white wine and reduce for about 5 minutes.
3. Add beef broth and bring to a boil. Reduce heat and simmer for 20 minutes.
4. Season with salt and pepper.
5. Toast bread slices until golden brown.
6. Place toasted bread in soup bowls, pour soup over bread, and top with grated Gruyere.
7. Broil in the oven until cheese is melted and bubbly.
8. Serve hot.

7. Butternut Squash and Sage Soup

- Preparation Time: 15 minutes
- Cooking Time: 30 minutes
- Servings: 4

Ingredients:

- 1 butternut squash, peeled and cubed
- 1 onion, chopped
- 3 cloves garlic, minced
- 4 cups vegetable broth
- 2 tbsp fresh sage, chopped
- 1/2 cup heavy cream (optional for richness)
- 2 tbsp olive oil
- Salt and pepper, to taste

Directions:

1. Heat olive oil in a large pot over medium heat. Add onion and garlic, sautéing until soft.
2. Add butternut squash and vegetable broth. Bring to a boil, then reduce heat and simmer until squash is tender, about 20 minutes.
3. Puree the soup with an immersion blender until smooth.
4. Stir in chopped sage and heavy cream (if using). Heat through.
5. Season with salt and pepper.
6. Serve hot.

8. Tomato Basil Soup

- Preparation Time: 10 minutes
- Cooking Time: 30 minutes
- Servings: 4

Ingredients:

- 1 can (28 oz) whole peeled tomatoes
- 1 onion, chopped
- 3 cloves garlic, minced
- 1/2 cup fresh basil, chopped
- 2 cups vegetable broth
- 1/2 cup heavy cream (optional for richness)
- 2 tbsp olive oil
- Salt and pepper, to taste

Directions:

1. Heat olive oil in a pot over medium heat. Add onion and garlic, cooking until onion is translucent.
2. Add tomatoes with their juices and vegetable broth. Bring to a boil, then reduce heat and simmer for about 20 minutes.

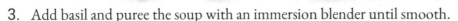

3. Add basil and puree the soup with an immersion blender until smooth.
4. Stir in heavy cream if using and heat through.
5. Season with salt and pepper.
6. Serve hot, garnished with additional basil if desired.

9. Chickpea and Spinach Stew

- Preparation Time: 10 minutes
- Cooking Time: 20 minutes
- Servings: 4

Ingredients:
- 1 can (15 oz) chickpeas, rinsed and drained
- 4 cups fresh spinach
- 1 onion, chopped
- 2 cloves garlic, minced
- 1 tsp ground cumin
- 1 tsp smoked paprika
- 2 tbsp tomato paste
- 3 cups vegetable broth
- 2 tbsp olive oil
- Salt and pepper, to taste

Directions:
1. Heat olive oil in a large pot over medium heat. Add onion and garlic, cooking until soft.
2. Stir in cumin and paprika, cooking for another minute until fragrant.
3. Add chickpeas, tomato paste, and vegetable broth. Bring to a boil, then reduce heat and simmer for 10 minutes.
4. Add spinach and cook until wilted, about 5 minutes.
5. Season with salt and pepper.
6. Serve hot.

10. Zucchini and Basil Velouté

- Preparation Time: 10 minutes
- Cooking Time: 20 minutes
- Servings: 4

Ingredients:
- 3 zucchinis, sliced
- 1 potato, peeled and cubed
- 1 onion, chopped
- 3 cups vegetable broth
- 1/4 cup fresh basil, chopped
- 1/4 cup heavy cream (optional)

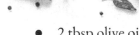

- 2 tbsp olive oil
- Salt and pepper, to taste

Directions:

1. Heat olive oil in a large pot over medium heat. Add onion and cook until translucent.
2. Add zucchini and potato, cooking for a few minutes until slightly softened.
3. Pour in vegetable broth and bring to a boil. Reduce heat and simmer until vegetables are tender, about 15 minutes.
4. Add basil and puree the soup until smooth using an immersion blender.
5. Stir in heavy cream if using, and heat through.
6. Season with salt and pepper.
7. Serve hot, garnished with more fresh basil if desired.

11. Cauliflower and Turmeric Soup

- Preparation Time: 10 minutes
- Cooking Time: 25 minutes
- Servings: 4

Ingredients:

- 1 head cauliflower, chopped
- 1 onion, chopped
- 3 cloves garlic, minced
- 1 tsp turmeric
- 4 cups vegetable broth
- 1/2 cup coconut milk
- 2 tbsp olive oil
- Salt and pepper, to taste

Directions:

1. Heat olive oil in a large pot over medium heat. Add onion and garlic, sautéing until onion is translucent.
2. Stir in turmeric and cook for another minute.
3. Add cauliflower and vegetable broth. Bring to a boil, then reduce heat and simmer until cauliflower is tender, about 20 minutes.
4. Puree the soup with an immersion blender until smooth.
5. Stir in coconut milk and heat through.
6. Season with salt and pepper.
7. Serve hot.

12. Sweet Potato and Ginger Soup

- Preparation Time: 10 minutes
- Cooking Time: 25 minutes
- Servings: 4

Ingredients:

- 2 sweet potatoes, peeled and cubed
- 1 onion, chopped
- 2 inches fresh ginger, peeled and minced
- 4 cups vegetable broth
- 1/2 cup coconut milk
- 2 tbsp olive oil
- Salt and pepper, to taste

Directions:

1. Heat olive oil in a large pot over medium heat. Add onion and ginger, cooking until onion is soft.
2. Add sweet potatoes and vegetable broth. Bring to a boil, then reduce heat and simmer until sweet potatoes are tender, about 20 minutes.
3. Puree the soup with an immersion blender until smooth.
4. Stir in coconut milk and heat through.
5. Season with salt and pepper.
6. Serve hot.

13. Carrot and Coriander Soup

- Preparation Time: 10 minutes
- Cooking Time: 30 minutes
- Servings: 4

Ingredients:

- 6 carrots, peeled and sliced
- 1 onion, chopped
- 1 bunch fresh coriander, chopped
- 4 cups vegetable broth
- 1/2 cup cream (optional)
- 2 tbsp olive oil
- Salt and pepper, to taste

Directions:

1. Heat olive oil in a pot over medium heat. Add onion and cook until soft.
2. Add carrots and cook for a few minutes until they start to soften.
3. Pour in vegetable broth and bring to a boil. Reduce heat and simmer until carrots are very tender, about 20 minutes.
4. Add most of the coriander, reserving some for garnish.

5. Puree the soup in the pot with an immersion blender until smooth.
6. Stir in cream if using, and heat through.
7. Season with salt and pepper.
8. Serve hot, garnished with the reserved coriander.

14. Beetroot and Potato Soup

- Preparation Time: 15 minutes
- Cooking Time: 35 minutes
- Servings: 4

Ingredients:
- 3 beets, peeled and diced
- 2 potatoes, peeled and diced
- 1 onion, chopped
- 4 cups vegetable broth
- 1/2 cup sour cream (optional)
- 2 tbsp olive oil
- Salt and pepper, to taste

Directions:
1. Heat olive oil in a large pot over medium heat. Add onion and cook until translucent.
2. Add beets and potatoes, cooking for a few minutes until they begin to soften.
3. Pour in vegetable broth and bring to a boil. Reduce heat and simmer until beets and potatoes are tender, about 30 minutes.
4. Puree the soup with an immersion blender until smooth.
5. Stir in sour cream if using, and heat through.
6. Season with salt and pepper.
7. Serve hot.

15. Pumpkin and Cinnamon Soup

- Preparation Time: 10 minutes
- Cooking Time: 30 minutes
- Servings: 4

Ingredients:
- 1 small pumpkin, peeled and cubed
- 1 onion, chopped
- 1 tsp ground cinnamon
- 4 cups vegetable broth
- 1/2 cup cream (optional)
- 2 tbsp olive oil
- Salt and pepper, to taste

Directions:

1. Heat olive oil in a large pot over medium heat. Add onion and cook until soft.
2. Add pumpkin and cinnamon, cooking for a few more minutes to allow the flavors to meld.
3. Pour in vegetable broth and bring to a boil. Reduce heat and simmer until pumpkin is tender, about 25 minutes.
4. Puree the soup with an immersion blender until smooth.
5. Stir in cream if using, and heat through.
6. Season with salt and pepper.
7. Serve hot, garnished with a sprinkle of cinnamon if desired.

16. Spicy Tomato and Red Pepper Soup

- Preparation Time: 10 minutes
- Cooking Time: 30 minutes
- Servings: 4

Ingredients:

- 4 large tomatoes, chopped
- 2 red bell peppers, chopped
- 1 onion, chopped
- 2 cloves garlic, minced
- 1 tsp crushed red pepper flakes
- 4 cups vegetable broth
- 2 tbsp olive oil
- Salt and pepper, to taste

Directions:

1. Heat olive oil in a large pot over medium heat. Add onion and garlic, cooking until onion is translucent.
2. Add tomatoes, red bell peppers, and red pepper flakes, cooking for a few more minutes until vegetables start to soften.
3. Pour in vegetable broth and bring to a boil. Reduce heat and simmer for 20 minutes.
4. Puree the soup with an immersion blender until smooth.
5. Season with salt and pepper.
6. Serve hot, garnished with a dollop of yogurt or sour cream if desired.

17. Barley and Mushroom Stew

- Preparation Time: 15 minutes
- Cooking Time: 45 minutes
- Servings: 4

Ingredients:

- 1 cup pearl barley, rinsed
- 1 lb mushrooms, sliced
- 1 onion, chopped
- 2 cloves garlic, minced
- 4 cups vegetable broth
- 2 tbsp olive oil
- 1/4 cup fresh parsley, chopped
- Salt and pepper, to taste

Directions:

1. Heat olive oil in a large pot over medium heat. Add onion and garlic, sautéing until onion is translucent.
2. Add mushrooms and cook until they release their juices and begin to brown.
3. Stir in barley and vegetable broth. Bring to a boil, then reduce heat and simmer, covered, for about 40 minutes, or until barley is tender.
4. Season with salt and pepper.
5. Stir in fresh parsley just before serving.
6. Serve hot.

Sweet Treats and Healthy Snacks

1. Greek Yogurt with Honey and Nuts

- Preparation Time: 5 minutes
- Cooking Time: 0 minutes
- Servings: 2

Ingredients:

- 2 cups Greek yogurt
- 4 tbsp honey
- 1/2 cup mixed nuts, chopped

Directions:

1. Divide the yogurt between two bowls.
2. Drizzle each bowl with 2 tablespoons of honey.
3. Sprinkle chopped nuts on top.
4. Serve immediately for a creamy and satisfying snack.

2. Fig and Walnut Bites

- Preparation Time: 15 minutes
- Cooking Time: 0 minutes
- Servings: 4

Ingredients:

- 12 dried figs, stems removed
- 1/2 cup walnuts
- 1/4 cup cream cheese
- 1 tbsp orange zest

Directions:

1. Slice each fig halfway through from the top.
2. In a food processor, blend walnuts until finely chopped.
3. Mix chopped walnuts with cream cheese and orange zest until well combined.
4. Stuff each fig with the walnut mixture.
5. Serve as a sweet, nutritious treat.

3. Almond and Date Energy Balls

- Preparation Time: 10 minutes
- Cooking Time: 0 minutes
- Servings: 10 balls

Ingredients:

- 1 cup dates, pitted
- 1/2 cup almonds
- 1/4 cup shredded coconut
- 1 tbsp cocoa powder

Directions:

1. Place dates and almonds in a food processor and blend until a sticky mixture forms.
2. Add cocoa powder and continue to blend until incorporated.
3. Roll the mixture into small balls.
4. Coat each ball in shredded coconut.
5. Refrigerate for at least 30 minutes before serving.

4. Baked Pear with Cinnamon

- Preparation Time: 5 minutes
- Cooking Time: 25 minutes
- Servings: 4

Ingredients:

- 4 pears, halved and cored
- 2 tsp cinnamon
- 4 tsp honey
- A few drops of lemon juice

Directions:

1. Preheat the oven to 350°F (175°C).
2. Place pear halves on a baking sheet.
3. Sprinkle each pear half with cinnamon and a few drops of lemon juice.
4. Drizzle each with a teaspoon of honey.
5. Bake in the preheated oven for 25 minutes, or until pears are soft and slightly caramelized.
6. Serve warm.

5. Avocado Chocolate Mousse

- Preparation Time: 10 minutes
- Cooking Time: 0 minutes
- Servings: 4

Ingredients:

- 2 ripe avocados

- 1/4 cup cocoa powder
- 1/4 cup honey or maple syrup
- 1 tsp vanilla extract
- A pinch of salt

Directions:

1. Scoop the flesh from the avocados and place it in a blender.
2. Add cocoa powder, honey or maple syrup, vanilla extract, and salt.
3. Blend until the mixture is smooth and creamy.
4. Chill in the refrigerator for at least 1 hour before serving.

6. Olive Tapenade with Whole Grain Crackers

- Preparation Time: 10 minutes
- Cooking Time: 0 minutes
- Servings: 4

Ingredients:

- 1 cup pitted Kalamata olives
- 1 tbsp capers
- 2 cloves garlic
- 2 tbsp olive oil
- Juice of 1/2 lemon
- Whole grain crackers, for serving

Directions:

1. In a food processor, combine olives, capers, garlic, olive oil, and lemon juice.
2. Blend until the mixture forms a coarse paste.
3. Serve with whole grain crackers for dipping.

7. Zucchini Chips

- Preparation Time: 10 minutes
- Cooking Time: 2 hours
- Servings: 4

Ingredients:

- 2 zucchinis, thinly sliced
- 2 tbsp olive oil
- Salt, to taste

Directions:

1. Preheat the oven to 225°F (105°C).
2. Toss zucchini slices in olive oil and salt.
3. Arrange slices in a single layer on a baking sheet.
4. Bake in the preheated oven for 2 hours, flipping the slices halfway through, until crispy and golden.

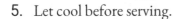

5. Let cool before serving.

8. Mediterranean Stuffed Dates

- Preparation Time: 15 minutes
- Cooking Time: 0 minutes
- Servings: 4

Ingredients:
- 16 Medjool dates, pitted
- 1/2 cup goat cheese
- 1/4 cup chopped walnuts
- 1/4 cup honey
- A pinch of sea salt

Directions:
1. Carefully slit each date on one side to create an opening.
2. Fill each date with a small amount of goat cheese and chopped walnuts.
3. Drizzle with honey and sprinkle a tiny bit of sea salt on top.
4. Serve as a sweet and savory snack.

9. Fresh Fruit Salad with Mint and Lime

- Preparation Time: 15 minutes
- Cooking Time: 0 minutes
- Servings: 4

Ingredients:
- 2 cups mixed fresh fruits (such as berries, melon, and kiwi)
- Juice of 1 lime
- 1 tbsp honey
- 1/4 cup fresh mint, chopped

Directions:
1. In a large bowl, combine all the fresh fruits.
2. In a small bowl, whisk together lime juice and honey.
3. Pour the dressing over the fruits and gently toss to coat.
4. Sprinkle with chopped mint before serving.

10. Roasted Chickpeas

- Preparation Time: 5 minutes
- Cooking Time: 30 minutes
- Servings: 4

Ingredients:
- 1 can (15 oz) chickpeas, rinsed and drained

- 2 tbsp olive oil
- 1 tsp smoked paprika
- Salt and pepper, to taste

Directions:

1. Preheat the oven to 400°F (200°C).
2. Pat chickpeas dry with paper towels and toss them in a bowl with olive oil, smoked paprika, salt, and pepper.
3. Spread chickpeas in a single layer on a baking sheet.
4. Roast in the preheated oven for 30 minutes, stirring occasionally, until crispy and golden.
5. Let cool before serving.

11. Ricotta and Berry Parfait

- Preparation Time: 10 minutes
- Cooking Time: 0 minutes
- Servings: 4

Ingredients:

- 2 cups ricotta cheese
- 2 cups mixed berries (such as strawberries, blueberries, and raspberries)
- 4 tbsp almond slices, toasted
- 4 tsp honey

Directions:

1. In serving glasses, layer ricotta cheese, mixed berries, and toasted almonds.
2. Drizzle each parfait with honey.
3. Serve immediately or chill until ready to serve.

12. Grilled Peaches with Balsamic Glaze

- Preparation Time: 5 minutes
- Cooking Time: 10 minutes
- Servings: 4

Ingredients:

- 4 peaches, halved and pitted
- 2 tbsp balsamic vinegar
- 2 tbsp honey
- 1/2 cup Greek yogurt, for serving

Directions:

1. Preheat the grill to medium-high heat.
2. In a small bowl, mix balsamic vinegar and honey.
3. Brush the cut side of the peaches with the balsamic mixture.
4. Grill peaches, cut side down, for about 5 minutes, then flip and grill for another 5 minutes until tender and caramelized.

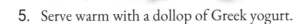

5. Serve warm with a dollop of Greek yogurt.

13. Spiced Orange Slices

- Preparation Time: 10 minutes
- Cooking Time: 0 minutes
- Servings: 4

Ingredients:
- 4 oranges, peeled and sliced into rounds
- 1 tsp cinnamon
- 1/2 tsp nutmeg
- 2 tbsp honey

Directions:
1. Arrange orange slices on a serving platter.
2. Sprinkle with cinnamon and nutmeg.
3. Drizzle with honey.
4. Serve immediately or let sit for a few minutes to allow flavors to meld.

14. Sesame Honey Bars

- Preparation Time: 10 minutes
- Cooking Time: 20 minutes
- Servings: 12 bars

Ingredients:
- 1 cup sesame seeds
- 1/2 cup honey
- 1/4 cup sugar
- 1 tsp vanilla extract

Directions:
1. In a saucepan over medium heat, combine honey and sugar. Cook until the sugar has dissolved and the mixture is bubbling.
2. Stir in sesame seeds and vanilla extract, mixing until the seeds are thoroughly coated.
3. Pour the mixture into a lined baking tray, spreading evenly.
4. Allow to cool completely before cutting into bars.

15. Walnut Stuffed Figs

- Preparation Time: 10 minutes
- Cooking Time: 0 minutes
- Servings: 4

Ingredients:

- 12 dried figs
- 1/2 cup walnuts
- 1/4 cup mascarpone cheese
- Honey, for drizzling

Directions:

1. Make a small incision in each fig without cutting through completely.
2. Stuff each fig with a small amount of mascarpone cheese and a walnut.
3. Arrange on a platter and drizzle with honey.
4. Serve as a decadent yet healthy treat.

16. Pistachio and Cranberry Bites

- Preparation Time: 15 minutes
- Cooking Time: 0 minutes
- Servings: 10 bites

Ingredients:

- 1 cup pistachios, shelled
- 1/2 cup dried cranberries
- 1/4 cup coconut flakes
- 2 tbsp honey

Directions:

1. In a food processor, pulse pistachios, cranberries, and coconut flakes until coarsely ground.
2. Add honey and pulse until the mixture starts to clump together.
3. Roll into small balls.
4. Refrigerate for at least 30 minutes before serving.

17. Apple Slices with Almond Butter

- Preparation Time: 5 minutes
- Cooking Time: 0 minutes
- Servings: 4

Ingredients:

- 2 apples, cored and sliced
- 1/2 cup almond butter
- Cinnamon, for sprinkling

Directions:

1. Spread almond butter on each apple slice.
2. Sprinkle with cinnamon.
3. Serve immediately or chill in the refrigerator before enjoying.

If you've enjoyed reading this book, I'd be incredibly grateful if you could spare a moment to leave a review. Your feedback doesn't just help other readers discover new adventures; it's also essential for independent authors like myself to grow and refine our craft.

Simply scan the QR Code below to leave your review:

Your review truly can make a difference. Thank you so much for your support!

Made in the USA
Las Vegas, NV
13 December 2024

14146797R00066